001668

780·92/BEE

THE UNCONSCIOUS BEETHOVEN

BY THE SAME AUTHOR:

GLUCK AND THE OPERA
WAGNER AS MAN AND ARTIST

THE
UNCONSCIOUS
BEETHOVEN

ERNEST NEWMAN

AN ESSAY

IN MUSICAL PSYCHOLOGY

With an Introduction by
Neville Cardus

REVISED EDITION

LONDON
VICTOR GOLLANCZ LTD
1968

575 00167 4

Printed in Great Britain by
Lowe & Brydone (Printers) Ltd., London

CONTENTS

INTRODUCTION

by Neville Cardus

INTRODUCTION

I IMAGINE that during Ernest Newman's lifetime I was his most constant and persistent reader. I became acquainted with his writings for the first time in 1907, when I had just celebrated my eighteenth birthday; and I read the last article that came from his pen before it dropped from his hand. He had then achieved, like Faust, his ninety years. I mention Goethe's *Faust*, in the Newman context, because it was his essay on " Faust in Music ", contained in his *Musical Studies*, published in 1905, which first put me in touch with his mind and attitude to criticism. I found the book in a Manchester Free Library; and to this day I remember stopping under a street lamp to read:

> Goethe, in fact, made the subject an essentially modern one — put into it the fever and the fret, the finer joys and the more impassioned spiritual aspirations, of the generations that succeeded the great upheaval of the eighteenth century. . . . The cosmic quality of the subject, one would think, should have attracted more of the first-rank men, considering how many of the second-rate it has tempted to self-destruction. One wonders, for example, why it should have fallen to the lot of Gounod to give so many honest but uninstructed people their first, perhaps their only, idea of *Faust*.

These words came to me as a shock and as a revelation, I revelled in Gounod's opera as an opera; but I saw Newman's point with youthful intuition. The essay introduced me to Goethe, and it wasn't the practice, or habit, half-a-century ago, of music critics to refer parenthetically to the masterpieces of literature. Newman's first approach to music was, in fact, blessedly indirect; at any rate, his writings on music ran parallel with an intensive study of sociology and kindred subjects. He contributed to J. M. Robertson's *Free Review*, severely rationalist. He went, with his genius for controversy, into the Weismann-Lamarck argument about inherited characteristics. He bludgeoned Herbert Spencer, during the philosopher's lifetime; Spencer had ventured a theory of the " Origin of Music ", which Newman, still in his twenties, would have nothing of. Newman was actually only in his twenty-seventh year when his erudite *Gluck and the Opera* was published in 1895. In it he outlined his critical *rationale* : the critic should keep his eye on the physiology of a composition, relating it to its cultural environment, and so on. " It is perfectly futile," wrote the young Ernest, " to go on discussing the aesthetic of music *in abstracto*, without reference to the historical conditions under which the art has lived and by which it has been moulded from century to century." He expounded and elaborated continuously his first principle of criticism: music *qua* music. Not, of course, as a thing in itself : the extra-musical connotations are there, but not as an emotional by-product, rather as integral *musical* shaping and germinating forces. In his book *The Unconscious Beethoven* this probing principle of Newman's is at work at its most searching.

He was a nobly Faustian searcher: he pursued " the object as in itself it really is ". He was not interested in the critic who went adventuring imaginatively among the masterpieces, only to describe his personal subjective reactions. He called me (affectionately), " a sensitized plate ". " The chief object of the critic," he maintained, " is to get other people to see the thing as he sees it; in other words, to get us to believe that he is right in calling this work good and the other bad. And how is this appeal of his judgment to ours to succeed unless he and we agree on certain standards of goodness, or rightness, that are independent of our little subjectivities? " There is a passage somewhere in his prolific output, in which he says: " No critic who thinks at all about his work can feel anything but depression after twenty or so years at it " — a sad cry from the heart, which reminds me of Faust's despairing sigh, " *Habe nun ach* ! *Philosophie*." Newman, who distrusted the critical antennae of a " sensitized plate ", asserted that " there is no more expressive choral writing in Europe today, than Granville Bantock's " (*circa* 1910); that Josef Holbrooke's four symphonic-poems " will one day be recognized as something new in English music or in any other music. They have an atmosphere, a psychology, that are his own and his alone. They are not imitative ; this atmosphere and this psychology are not in Wagner or Tchaikovsky, or Richard Strauss. . . ." He wrote of the " Domestic " Symphony of Strauss in 1905 that " I take it to be the work of an enormously clever man who was once a genius." *Once* a genius, mark you! — and all the best of Strauss to come. I confess that I enjoyed the irony of it all ; the " scientific " radar was no more to be trusted to avoid human error than all the plungings into

subjective deeps by the "sensitized plate" swimmer —
who, at any rate, did know something of the technique
of swimming.

The fact is, it is almost needless to say, Newman was
far beyond the control of a " scientific method "
derived from Hennequin, Taine and the rest. He was a
full man, temperament, intellect, nerve and blood
stream in proportion. In his heyday he was as prone as
the least " scientific " to let his personal reactions go
unleashed. For example:

> Heaven knows how empty some of these instrumental works
> of Mozart can be! The G minor symphony has more
> Eingeweide in it, but even here, one sometimes felt that we
> were merely listening to the nursery prattle of a bright child.
> . . . It is the correct thing, of course, to lament the passing of
> Mozart — or at all events of a good deal of his work — and
> to cry that something has gone out of music that will never
> return. It may be so; but, on the other hand, a great deal
> has come in that Mozart never dreamt of; and modern
> music has gained infinitely more than it has lost. One needed
> only to pass to the Strauss "Burleske" for piano and orchestra
> to realize this.

The Strauss "Burleske", milked Brahms and immature,
if brisk Strauss, set against the G minor symphony! O
he did it all as any " sensitized plate " as ever I knew!
— to echo the admiring cry of the Hostess of Falstaff.
Newman, in fact, sowed his wild sensitized oats freely
and gaily enough in his younger years. Post-Hitler-war
London knew him only in his maturity. When he was
critic in Birmingham he was called a " living and walk-
ing indiscretion ". The staid pages of the *Post* had ample

cause daily to be shocked. " The higher the voice, the lower the intellect," he wrote of Melba. Of a quartet by a revered London academical composer, a very academical and prolific composer, Newman made excuses for it thus: " Judging by the Opus number, 259, obviously an early work." *He* was in those days as likely as myself to let objectivity go hang, in a grand flush of personal reaction, and write of Scriabine's " Prometheus " in this empurpled way:

> The wind that blows through this music is the veritable wind of the cosmos itself; the cries of desire and passion and ecstasy are a sort of quintessential sublimation of all the yearnings, not merely of humanity but of all nature animate and inanimate. . . .

I have had my private chuckles about the change of the Newman of his Birmingham days to the Newman who metamorphosed to the Sage of Tadworth, a conversion like that of the sower of critical wild oats who, having had a good time with all manner of joyful subjective profligacies, warns us in his closing decades of the dangerous way that deviates from self-denying detachment and the strait and narrow path of sober objectivity.

Newman's quest after the Absolute was one of the noblest efforts in the music-criticism of our age. As a man increases his wisdom and experience, and becomes aware of the difference between appearance and the substance behind it which we are driven presumptuously to call reality, he wearies of messages communicated to the senses and emotions; indeed, his capacity for sensory and emotional participation is probably wearing thin. He seeks for first causes; he wants to get to the root of the matter. Newman was right to protest against the kind of writing which, on the one hand, is extra-musical, " literature " at its best, irrelevant to germinal stuff and organized structure; and on the other, is merely analytical, describing the technical and stylistic means, but saying nothing illuminating about the aesthetic end. " Show me the *mind* of Beethoven at work," he implored, " I am not interested in what you, apropos Beethoven, reveal of yourself."

Most of us are content to systematize our own reactions to music, intellectual and emotional. For my own part, I have found the task hard enough to clarify and rationalize my personal *experiences* as a listener to music. Critical truth, seen *sub specie aeternetatis*, has never been my aim. Newman was a born advocate, and naturally, he set himself to convince, to prove his case. His quest was all the more self-denying because, as he himself once put it, " the critic is even more painfully the product of his epoch than the composer. He is blinded by the dust of the fights that are raging round him; he cannot see problems and principles but only individuals and antagonisms."

In his high noon of life he was a cosmopolitan of the world of civilized men and women, black of hair, like a latter-day Disraeli. His walk had a springy easy poise, which was something of a physical manifestation of the way his mind and sensibility moved and worked. Though he turned often and naturally to German ways of thinking, in music and in literature, and though he could happily spend summer months at Bayreuth in the company of obsessive Wagnerians, he was, *au fond*, Latin in the volatility of his temperament, and in the precision of his writing and dialectic. He could modulate easefully from Bayreuth to Monte Carlo, from the B minor Mass to Offenbach, from Covent Garden Opera to a boxing-fight at the Royal Albert Hall. His wit could go to the point like a rapier, tinctured by humour. He had me in disgrace one night at Covent Garden, at a performance of *Parsifal*, by a remark which erupted from me a guffaw that provoked the entire stalls to a vehement " Shush! " Weingartner was conducting, and his *tempi* got slower and slower, arriving more or less at a standstill during the " Good Friday " music. Newman, seated in front of me, turned round and whispered, " Cardus, before this ' Good Friday' music is at an end it'll be Easter Monday." We were passing through Leicester Square one summer evening in the period of the street-walking Ladies of Joy. A man on a soap-box near the gardens was calling on his audience to come and be saved. A number of these Ladies of Joy dallied on the small crowd's fringe, listening. " Look," said Newman, " look — St. Francis preaching to the birds. . . ."

Anybody with a comprehensive mind and consciousness as full as Newman's, living his great length of life, is bound to go through metamorphoses of intellectual awareness and psychological responses. In his ninety years, Newman might easily have fulfilled himself greatly as (1) the most perceptive and humane English critic of literature since Hazlitt or Coleridge, (2) as a biologist, (3) as an advocate or an attorney-general, and

(4) as an all-round journalist as accomplished as Alistair Cooke. In his mid-twenties he could write this way about Amiel:

> It is the voice of Geneva speaking; and the thing is that it should come from the mouth of a man who is at other times partly Schopenhauer, Hegel, Stoic, Epicurean and Oriental quietist. The dualism of Amiel's nature was his destruction; he cannot harmonize everything within him, and yet tortures himself because of his failure, ultimately seeking a fictitious harmonization by strangling philosophy in the arms of religion. Geneva is at the bottom of him, suggesting dark problems of sin, and evil, and death, and salvation. And since he cannot attain the inward peace he strives for, and since he cannot flout God in the face, and show him the cardinal blunder he has made in the clumsy creation of mankind, he takes a thin ascetic comfort in the Christian theory of the innate perversity of man, ad radicale Böse of Kant . . .

Of George Meredith (written in 1903, bear in mind):

> It may not seem very illuminating to say that he is too imaginative to be a convincing realist, even in his own sense of the word. Nevertheless, an examination of some of the mental qualities underlying his style may throw a little fresh light on the formula. When I say that it is Mr. Meredith's imagination that makes his treatment of life unconvincing, I mean that he is so much the slave of a verbal faculty that is always getting unmanageable at the slightest suggestion from his fancy, as to be incapable of producing life as he has seen it. The imaginative mind fastens upon each impression as it appears, and gives it out again coloured by the reflection upon it of light from other impressions. But this faculty of spon-

taneous co-ordination needs to be held in check by a higher
nervous centre; and in Mr. Meredith this superior control is
decidedly lacking. Not only is his verbal faculty extremely
opulent in itself, but it is always liable to be overcharged by
the influx of irrelevant suggestions from his imagination, that
groups together, in one lightning flash, things that are sometimes only distantly related. . . .

Newman's forensic agility was demonstrated during
the debate with Bernard Shaw in the *Nation* of March
1910, when the two men disagreed over Richard
Strauss's *Elektra*. Shaw admitted that he was several
times " pinked " by Newman's rapier.

His propensity as a biologist, looking into germ-
plasm and the evolving structure, is forcibly demonstrated in this new edition of his *Unconscious Beethoven*.
And his born aptitude as an all-round journalist was
proven by his vivid description of the historic boxing
fight in the Royal Albert Hall, London, when Carpen-
tier fought (I think) Johnson; he reviewed the
encounter, "on the night", for the *Manchester Guardian*.
At any time, Newman could have deputized for the
principal leader-writer, and argued any liberal case
of politics, ethics, morals, finance — and whatever.
Another ironical curiosity about Newman is that *he*,
who was so emphatic that music should be studied,
listened to, and written about *qua* music, frequently
approached a composition first as biologist or psycho-
logist, and only secondarily from the aesthetic point of
view.

Also — I had nearly forgotten — yet another facet
of the mental equipment of this encyclopaedic man:

he might well have achieved eminence as a historian. His four-volume biography of Wagner out-Thayers Thayer's *Beethoven* in point of vast and pertinent documentation; and, of course, it is far better written. The energy of his mind was tireless; his appetite for knowledge never staled. On his deathbed he asked that records of *Parsifal* be played to him, and after concentrating intently, said: " I must get well, you know — some new ideas about *Parsifal* have just occurred to me." For half a century he produced a weekly column, as freshly and apparently as easily written at the end as at the beginning. I can close my tribute to him now in no words more sincere, and grateful, than those I wrote for the *Fanfare for Ernest Newman*, edited by Herbert Van Thal, some years ago.

" Only those who began to read and study Newman as young men can understand how much is owed to him in this country for his work in enriching and fructifying an atmosphere and soil during an acrid time of provincial stuffiness and narrowness of vision. He was perhaps the first writer truly to Europeanize our music, and our human responses to music. He quickened our antennae, opened doors for us."

THE UNCONSCIOUS BEETHOVEN

FOREWORD TO THE SECOND EDITION

*I*T *is a not uncommon practice for an author to
reply, in a second edition of his book, to criticisms
of the first. But no preface should be longer than
the book itself; and if I were to reply in detail to the
criticisms of the present little volume I should have
the air of placing a portico in front of a cottage
several sizes too small for it. I must content myself
with a brief indication of the line some of my critics
took, and of my own view of their contributions to
the subject.*

*Criticism was mainly directed against two of my
theses. I had ventured to surmise that certain curious phases of Beethoven's mentality in his later
years may have been the product of his syphilis.
Thereupon a number of writers, of whom Mr. Carl
Engel was probably the ablest and certainly the
most voluble, sought to confute me with the argument that there is no proof whatever that Beethoven's deafness was due to syphilis. They were
wasting their own, their readers', and my time.
Nothing is to be gained by reading what the medical*

men have to say about Beethoven's deafness. They all contradict each other, as is perhaps only to be expected in view of the fact that they are arguing about a case of which they have no first-hand experience. Schweisheimer plumps for an infection of the middle ear, not an otosclerosis. Bilancioni insists that it was otosclerosis. Marage (and with him Romain Rolland) rejects these and other theories in favour of one of his own — that Beethoven went deaf because he was an " over-strained intellectual." We may leave them arguing among themselves; their conclusions are of no interest to the rest of us one way or another.

It does not seem to have struck most of them, as it certainly has not struck Mr. Engel, that there is no need whatever to regard the syphilis and the deafness as being in the nature of cause and effect. The simple fact appears to have been overlooked that a man may have more than one thing the matter with him at the same time. If medical records were carefully examined, it would probably be found that it is by no means a rare thing for a man to have simultaneously astygmatism and corns; and there really seems no reason why we should put the astygmatism down to the corns, or the corns to the astygmatism. All the Beethoven investigators have been put on the wrong track by Lauder Brunton's declaration, some fifty years ago, that the state of Beethoven's auditory apparatus, as revealed by *the post-mortem, was " most probably the result of syphilitic affections at an early period of his life." Ever since then, discussions of the subject have taken the form of assertions on the one side that the deafness was the result of the syphilis, and on the other side that it was not; and the writers of the latter school of thought have jumped to the naive conclusion that if the auditory conditions could be shown to be accountable for on other grounds than those of syphilis, it was there and then established that Beethoven could not possibly have suffered from syphilis! It does not seem to have occurred to these bright intelligences — of whom Mr. Engel is a fair sample — that a man can both go deaf and contract syphilis, and that the two maladies may have no more causal connection with each other than astygmatism and corns have.*

If Mr. Engel will do me the honour to read my book again, this time when he is fully awake, he will discover that I have nowhere in it attributed Beethoven's deafness to syphilis; I had seen reason to give up that theory, which at one time I had accepted as blindly as other people had done. I am therefore quite untouched by Mr. Engel's declaration that " with our present knowledge, the only conclusion possible is that Beethoven's deafness was not caused by syphilis, either congenital or contracted." I have not said in my book that it was. I am indifferent to that matter one way or the other;

and Mr. Engel's elaborate medical lucubration has nothing to do with my thesis.

Whatever Mr. Engel may think, I hold it as a fairly safe conclusion, from all the evidence available, that Beethoven had contracted syphilis in his youth, and that the emotional and moral reactions that this disaster set up in him may account for certain of his actions in later life. As to the reasonableness of this view I leave it to the individual reader to decide. I hope to deal with the subject at greater length in a subsequent publication, and to give good reasons for thinking that the major misfortune is darkly hinted at by Beethoven himself in a document that has so far been misread.

The other main point on which my critics have fallen foul of me is the operation of the unconscious in Beethoven the composer. I was prepared for an exhibition of foolishness on this matter, but not for quite so much foolishness. More than one bright reviewer asked what was the final use of this demonstration of the processes by which Beethoven arrived at the first movement of his Eroica *symphony; will the knowledge of all this, I was asked, enable us to appreciate the* Eroica *one whit the more the next time we hear it? It will not. Nor will a knowledge of the marvellous mathematical relations between the walls and the angles of the honeycomb make the next spoonful of honey we take taste any sweeter in the mouth, or a knowledge of the*

*chemical principles by which nature has converted
mud and chlorophyll and other things into a rose
make us more sensitive to the scent of the next rose
we smell. Æsthetic enjoyment of a work of art is
not in the least dependent upon any knowledge of
the obscure mental processes that have gone to the
making of it; but that knowledge may be well worth
having for its own sake. If a man is not interested in
attempts of this kind to understand the subtle workings of the musical mind, there is no law to compel
him to read them. But he must not try to bar others
from making the attempt.*

*Objections were also raised to my putting for-
ward a certain ascending three-note sequence as a
" finger-print " of Beethoven. Reviewers who had
never given five minutes' thought in the whole
of their lives to the question of artists' " finger-
prints " had no hesitation in declaring that I was
merely the victim of my own fancy. Some of them
even pointed out that descending groups of three
notes are to be found in Beethoven! This discovery
that, in music, notes sometimes go down as well as
up is enough to immortalize any critic; and it is only
from motives of the basest professional jealousy, a
churlish reluctance to give credit where credit is
due, that I refrain from placing the names of these
Columbuses on record here. Mr. Engel, however, I
may say, is one of them. I venture to point out to all
these gentlemen that they have not quite grasped my*

argument. If a sequence of three descending notes can be shown to be used again and again by Beethoven in a particular way, it seems to my humble intelligence that so far from showing that the ascending sequence is not a "finger-print," it only shows the existence of yet another "finger-print." But the very essence of my exposition has been overlooked by these good people. Mr. Engel, for example, dogmatizing with all the confidence of the sciolist upon a matter he has manifestly never studied as it needs to be studied, sees in my "finger-print" only such a succession of notes as can be found all over the field of music; and he is rash enough to cite the ascent at the words "Es war ein herzig's Veilchen," in Mozart's song, as being on all fours with the quotations I have given from Beethoven. I cannot go over the whole ground again in this Foreword; I must content myself with referring the reader to the note on page 72 of the book, in which I answered in anticipation — for I well knew in advance what the sciolists would say — the shallow dogmatism of which Mr. Engel has given me so perfect an illustration.

Let me add, to be quite candid, that I now see that I was unwise in launching my views on the "finger-prints" of composers in this very incomplete form; my only excuse is that I wanted to clarify my own opinions on this complex subject by tentatively setting forth one of the simplest forms

*that the " finger-print " can take. After some twenty
years' research in this field, I have come to the conclusion that the idiom of each composer can be
shown to be based on quite a few formulæ, personal to that composer — and of course subtilisa-
tions of these formulæ — of which the man himself
is utterly unconscious. Having thrown out hints of
this in one or two articles, I was indignantly told
that I was reducing the composer to the rank of a
" machine." As it happens, however, the human and
animal body and brain show in a thousand ways
that they operate as machines over which the voli-
tion has no control. If I make as if to throw vitriol
into a man's eyes, a certain apparatus inside him
makes him close his eyes without his consciously
willing to do so. If a dog is cold, he huddles himself
together; if he is lying in a baking sun, he stretches
himself out to his fullest extent. Although he does
not know it, his object in the one case is to expose
as little of his body as possible to the radiation of its
own heat, in the other case to expose as much of his
surface as possible to radiation. There is a mecha-
nism in him that performs this adaptation of means
to ends without any consciousness of it on his part.
The unconscious — or, if we prefer the term, the
sub-conscious — operates incessantly in the human
mind as in the body; and I have devoted many years
of research to tracing these unconscious operations
in the work of composers. I hope to publish the*

results some day; and then, perhaps, it will be seen that such a " finger-print " as the little one of Beethoven's that I have cursorily touched upon in the present volume is not the fantastic invention that superficial readers have taken it to be.

E. N.

PART I

THE MAN

THE
UNCONSCIOUS BEETHOVEN

I

MR. PHILIP GUEDALLA has told us, in his pleasantly cynical way, that "patriotism and centenaries are the two greatest adversaries of the truth." The former can hardly be a danger to any but compatriots; but a centenary is always an ubiquitous temptation to indulge in rhapsody at the expense of veracity. The reason probably is that there is no sense in celebrating a centenary at all unless the subject of it is at least as important in the latter day as he was in his own; and the mere fact of his survival is held in many quarters to be sufficient justification for counting most of his hits at least twice and turning a blind eye to his misses. Yet it is precisely on the occasion of a centenary that we ought to try to see our subject as he really was. A centenary is, or should be, an opportunity for rediscovery. A great man's contemporaries see him, in the main, steadily if not whole; it is the business of the fourth or fifth generation after him to aim at wholeness without any loss of steadiness in the view. When the great man happens to be a composer the full significance of his work can be grasped only by a later age, because then only is it possible to see it in relation both to what preceded it and what came after it. Only the later age can discriminate between what was novel in his work that was of interest only for the moment and what was not only new but has proved seminal for his artistic posterity. Only a later age can see his work not merely in historical perspective but in what may be called personal perspective: to cite a single striking instance, Wagner's dramatic music, that was hailed with delight by the eager young spirits of his time as having set music free of the old hampering formalisms, can now be seen, even over so vast an expanse as the *Ring*, to be as formally organized as a classical symphony. Only a later age, again, can know, or approach to a knowledge of, the full greatness of a great artist, for his art is not simply and solely itself but what we, with our enlarged intellectual experience and intensified emotional life, can bring to it. But though no great artist can be as great for his own epoch as he is for later ones, his thoughtful contemporaries are perfectly well aware, in a general way, of his greatness, and in certain special ways are even more acutely aware of it than posterity is. For in the course of time, and especially in such an art as music, in which the vocabulary and the sonorous material develop in range from decade to decade, things that at their first appearance were overwhelmingly emotional tend to lose their nervous force and to become at the best the mere current coin of musical expression, and at the worst a currency that has become so depreciated that it will have to be called in. Certain pages of Beethoven that must have been an intoxication to the first hearers of them, the explosion of a nervous force that till then had been unknown in music, now seem to be the mere everyday speech of the art.

Musical criticism, in the full sense of the term, is not possible until the subject of it is separated from the critic by a hundred years at least, for only then can he see it through an approximately clear atmosphere. The first generation or two after a great artist's death inevitably sees him through a refracting medium of one kind or another. By one musical camp of the new time he is seen as the unconscious originator of what they feel to be the best in themselves: the Beethoven criticism of the Wagnerians of the mid-nineteenth century, for example, was unconsciously shaped and coloured by the desire to prove the Wagnerian music-drama to be the rightful heir of the Beethoven symphony, just as Wagner's own work was appealed to later as the begetter of the symphonic poems of Strauss and the songs of Hugo Wolf. Over against this camp there generally stands another which, desirous of " progress," sees in the great man of a generation or two before merely the quintessence of everything that is abhorrent to it, because his work clashes with its own conception of what music might be. It was thus that Mozart lay under a cloud here and there for a while in the early nineteenth century, and that Wagner, a few years ago, became the *bête noire* of certain schools that had little in common but a secret sense of impotence at the spectacle of this giant bestriding the main road of music. It is only in a much later period, when the great composer is of no practical use and no theoretical danger to either camp, that he can be seen without these atmospheric refractions; and when he is thus seen he looks, in certain essentials, very much as he did to his contemporaries. Historical criticism after a fairly long interval of time, indeed, is in some respects merely the clearing away from a monument of the dirt and rubbish — especially the romantic and sentimental rubbish — that have accumulated about it during the course of a century or so. At a certain stage of his posthumous career the great musician passes into the hands of the showmen-biographers, and, they being an incurably romantic-minded race, he generally emerges from their hands so changed that his contemporaries would hardly recognize him.

W E are not concerned, in this study, with Beethoven the man except in so far as the man throws
light on the musician; but as it is impossible to dissociate the two, we have as our first task to dig out
the real Beethoven from the romantic plaster-of-
Paris in which he has gradually become encased. Mr.
Krehbiel, in his new edition of Thayer's authorita-
tive biography, truly says that " it is doubtful if any
other great man's history has been so encrusted with
fiction as Beethoven's. Except Thayer's, no biography of him has been written which presents him in
his true light. The majority of the books which have
been written of late years repeat many of the errors
and falsehoods made current in the first books which
were written about him." At a very early stage a
Beethoven legend established itself, and the later
biographers went zealously about the traditional
business of polishing up this legend and eliminating
from it everything that did not harmonize with it.
This paralysis of the critical faculty extended, in
time, to his music. Beethoven became, for the late
nineteenth century, not a mere musician, the value
of whose work should be judged by the purely æsthetic tests we would apply to that of any other com-

poser, but a man with a message, a seer, an oracle
whose plenary inspiration on all occasions it were
blasphemy to doubt. His music was admired not
simply in terms of music but as an achievement in
morality. The humanitarian and democratic nineteenth century was so impressed by his choice of certain lofty literary subjects that it hardly occurred to
it to look critically at his manner of treating these
subjects in music. It was held, for example, to be
the sign of a particularly virtuous nature that he
should have chosen for the scene of his solitary
opera a story of conjugal fidelity. There had been a
regrettable tendency on the part of previous libret-
tists and composers of operas to take an interest in
characters, especially female characters, who would
hardly have been asked to tea by the most broad-
minded of Victorian rural deans; even in our own
day English writers have been known to assure us
solemnly that the subjects of *Don Giovanni* and
Figaro are "not edifying." But the Leonora of
Fidelio was respectable enough to be admitted into
any Victorian drawing-room: she could show her
marriage lines, she was not French, nothing was
known against the family, and she clung to her law-
ful spouse with an adoring fidelity that especially
appealed to Victorian male notions of the duty of
woman. "It" [*Fidelio*] "remains to this day," Sir
Charles Stanford could write, "the noblest, most
ideal, most human, most touching opera in exist-

ence." One already suspects that verdict to be
founded on moral rather than purely musical considerations, great as *Fidelio* is in its best moments;
and the suspicion becomes a certainty when we read
on a little further. The libretto " contained the germ
of the finest quality in human nature, self-sacrifice,
and provided him [Beethoven] with the means of
preaching a great sermon upon a small but piquant
text. A crust of bread has become in his hands the
means of stirring the world's emotions for a century." Even so acute and critical a musician as Stanford, we see, could allow his judgment of *Fidelio* to
be affected by moral and humanitarian considerations that are quite outside the domain of æsthetics.
Beethoven is praised not so much for the music he
has written to the opera as for having chosen a subject that was unimpeachable on the ground of morals. First of all we have the somewhat dubious *obiter
dictum* that self-sacrifice is " the finest quality in
human nature " — a sentiment of peculiar appeal to
the comfort-loving nineteenth century, that dearly
loved to read of self-sacrifice on the part of others
— and then, in some queer way, it is held to be a
point in Beethoven's favour as an artist that his
morals were sound, at any rate theoretically. It is a
doctrine that, pushed to its logical extreme, would
justify any bad oratorio written to any good Bible
text. As it happens, Beethoven's music to *Fidelio*
is often fine enough to justify all the praise we can

give it; but to regard a musical work as in any way
worthy of admiration merely because its text is
based on sound moral principles is to confuse æsthetics with morality. Many an eye has been blinded
with tears during the Prisoners' Chorus, not because of any particular quality in the music but
because the scene has struck home to the specta-
tor's humanitarian feelings : for the time being every
member of the audience has become a potential sub-
scribing member of the Howard Association.

This confusion of things æsthetic and things moral
was not applied to any other musical case than that
of Beethoven; there have been opera libretti before
and since that have lent themselves as readily to
sermons or to humanitarian propaganda as *Fidelio*,
but the composers of these had not the luck of Beethoven. They were judged solely and simply on their
achievements as musicians. Beethoven had his
peculiar luck partly because when *Fidelio* was estab-
lishing itself on the European stage Northern Europe was being bitten into deeply by what Nietzsche
called moralic acid, partly because, in one way and
another, he had succeeded in getting himself regarded posthumously as being of no less significance
to the universe as a moralist than as a composer.
The humanitarians of the nineteenth century grew
moist-eyed at the aspirations towards universal
brotherly love that are voiced in Schiller's *Ode to
Joy;* and in this emotional condition they declined,

as their successors still decline, to face fairly and squarely the question of the actual *musical* value of the choral ending of the Ninth Symphony. Beethoven's contemporaries, who had not yet had time to become poisoned with moralic acid, were under no illusions as to the general inferiority of this music to that of the main body of the work; while the Latin races, who are not so given as the Germans and the English to bemusing themselves with moral considerations where art is in question, steadily refused to accept Beethoven's inferior music merely because it came to them freighted with nebulous poetic talk about the gathering-in of the millions in one comprehensive embrace — Verdi, for instance, declaring that the Ninth Symphony is magnificent in the first three movements and much inferior in the last. As Debussy has said, " the Choral Symphony has been enveloped in a fog of high-sounding talk and epithets. It and the celebrated ' smile of La Gioconda,' to which there has become affixed forever the label of ' mysterious,' are the two masterpieces that have generated the greatest amount of foolish talk; one is astonished that the Symphony has not remained buried under the mass of prose it has called forth." Once more we have to recognize the curious fact that, alone among composers of secular music, Beethoven, over and above his virtues as a composer, has been credited with a special virtue as moralist.

III

I T is perhaps hardly surprising that this should be so, when we remember how even the man Beethoven became, during the nineteenth century, an idealized figure of personal morality. Everything helped the romanticizing biographers in their attempt to remake him in their own image — the peculiar grandeur of his music at its best, the pathos of his deafness, his many bodily miseries, his obvious unfitness for daily life as common men manage to live it. The conception gradually established itself of an earth-transcending seer, a sort of Tiresias whose affliction was not blindness but, still more tragic for a musician, deafness. Add to all this the fact that everybody who had come into conflict with him was seen by the obsequious biographers through Beethoven's hardly impartial eyes, and the further fact that the composer never lost an opportunity of bearing naïve testimony to his own vast moral superiority over other men, and it is hardly to be wondered at that, bit by bit, a fanciful Beethoven was constructed that bore the minimum of resemblance to Beethoven as he left his Maker's hands and as his contemporaries knew him. He became the subject of all sorts of romantic fictions invented to support the theory that

the man Beethoven who walked the streets of Vienna
habitually lived on the heights of ethical grandeur
that he attained in his mighty music. Everyone
knows the story of how, at one of the court hearings
in connection with the struggle for the guardianship
of his nephew, he was asked to produce documentary
proof of his nobility (the Dutch *van* not being regarded as the equivalent of the German *von*), whereupon he pointed to his head and his heart and said:
" My nobility is *here* and *here*." That, no doubt, is
what he ought to have said, and what, as the composer of the Fifth Symphony and the *Moonlight*
Sonata, he would have been fully entitled to say,
though a magistrates' court might still be pardoned
for having some doubts whether the composition of
these masterpieces was of itself sufficient assurance
of his qualifications to bring up a nephew. But there
is no evidence whatever that he made the remark.
Thayer [1] unearthed the shorthand notes of the case,
from which he publishes a number of extracts; and
we are driven to the conclusion either that this striking rejoinder of Beethoven was inexplicably excluded from the verbatim notes of the evidence, or
else, which is more probable, that he never made it,
but that it was the invention, long after the event, of
the regrettably unreliable Schindler.

---

[1] Here, as in all following references, " Thayer " means the three-
volume English edition of Thayer's biography as revised and completed,
from Thayer's papers, by Krehbiel. No useful purpose would be served
by attempting to allot this passage or that to one or other of the authors.

IV

AT almost every point the harsh — often splendidly harsh — lines of his character have been softened by the biographers; they have prettified and moralified and sublimized him as the sculptors and painters have mostly done. The latter show us nothing of the deep pock-marks that were among the first things that struck those who saw his face for the first time; while the ordinary second-hand biographers, long even after Thayer had so patiently unearthed the truth, persisted in depicting him as they conceived the composer of the Ninth Symphony and the Mass in D *must* have been — the one good man in a world of knaves and fools. Their treatment of the affair of the nephew is typical. The popular notion of this affair is that the one person wronged, and cruelly wronged, was Beethoven. That he suffered grievously through it, and that he conceived himself to be acting throughout from motives of the utmost purity, cannot be questioned. But men who are sure that their motives are, in the abstract, of the utmost purity, can sometimes attain that certitude by way of quite false premises, and in the attempt to realize their virtuous purpose can unconsciously do a great deal of harm.

There has been too easy-going an assumption that in everything that happened in this affair Beethoven was right and the others wrong — that he was in every way more fitted to be the guardian of Carl than the latter's mother was, and that Carl himself was a fundamentally bad boy who did nothing but plague his good uncle. The case did not present itself so simply to contemporary judges of it, nor does it so present itself to cool students of the evidence to-day. Beethoven set out with a hatred and distrust of his sister-in-law that can only be regarded as an obsession bordering on the insane. Later I shall hazard a possible explanation of this and similar obsessions on his part; here the bare facts need only be noted. At a certain point in his career the superb arrogance that his contemporaries all noted in him as a young man left the field of music and spread itself over that of life, especially other people's sexual life. He became, in plain words, a monomaniac, officiously interfering in the marital relations of his brothers. No aspect of him is so unpleasant as this.

Beethoven's brothers and his nephew have been especially badly treated by the conventional biographers, who, not knowing the man with whom they had to deal, put too much trust in Schindler. For three generations at least, sympathetic readers have wept over the story of how, when the composer's last illness was setting in, the nephew Carl was charged

to call in a doctor, and how, like the heartless young
wastrel he was, he forgot all about it until it happened to occur to him one day when he was play-
ing billiards, whereupon he nonchalantly asked the
marker to see about sending a doctor to his uncle.
The marker himself having fallen ill and been taken
to the hospital, so the story went on, he incidentally
mentioned the matter to the physician in charge,
Dr. Wawruch. Schindler boldly assured the world
that he had the story from Wawruch himself; but
Thayer says that this " story of unexampled heart-
lessness " is " branded as a shameless fabrication by
Dr. Wawruch's published statement and the evidence of the Conversation Book." The dates and
details given by Thayer prove the truth of this indictment. Thayer and Otto Jahn both knew Schindler personally in his old age, and having discussed
him together they came to the conclusion that he
was " honest and sincere in his statements, but af-
flicted with a treacherous memory and a proneness
to accept impressions and later-formed convictions
as facts of former personal knowledge, and to publish them as such without carefully verifying them."
There are times when one can only regard this judgment as erring considerably on the side of charity;
but be that as it may, there can be no doubt as to
Schindler's share in the responsibility for having
foisted upon the world the largely false picture of
Beethoven and his associates that is still current to-

day among biographers who, even yet, do not know their Thayer.

Beethoven's brothers, like his nephew, have been persistently denigrated in order to make a more effective background for his own supposed whiteness. Schindler made Beethoven's acquaintance in 1814. It was not till some years later that he came to know brother Johann, while there is no evidence that he ever knew brother Caspar at all.[1] Notwithstanding this, he did not hesitate, in the biography he published in 1840, to give his own account of events that happened, or were supposed to have happened, as early as 1800. If we assume that he derived his information, or part of it, from Beethoven himself, we have to remember that the composer, in whom suspicion of his friends and relations was at most times a positive mental and moral disease, is the most unreliable of witnesses where his brothers are concerned. Thayer is unusually severe on the biographers who, building upon and adding to the malicious conjectures of Schindler and others, have put into circulation a number of fictions concerning Johann and Caspar. They have represented the latter as " the seller of his wife's virtue and a sharer in the wages of her shame." The story, says Thayer " is utterly without foundation and a falsehood, and is

[1] The composer, born in 1770, was the eldest of the three brothers. Caspar Anton Carl was born in April, 1774, and died in 1815. Nikolaus Johann was born in October, 1776, and died in January, 1848. The nephew Carl (1807–1858) was the former's son.

told, moreover, of poor Caspar at a time when as yet he had no wife!" The brothers, calmly considered, seem to have been just ordinary human beings, no better and no worse than the rest of mankind, no better and no worse than the composer; " in a word," as Thayer says, " Beethoven was not a phenomenon of goodness, nor were his brothers monsters of iniquity."

V

BEETHOVEN'S colossal arrogance and self-suf-
ficiency, as I have said, were commented on by
everyone who knew him in his youth. They were the
natural expression of both a body and a musical
mind of exceptional power, and a power of which he
was magnificently conscious. Physically he was a
man of unusual strength even to the end. A score of
his contemporaries, among them more than one
physician, have left us their admiring testimony to
his splendid musculature and the toughness of his
bony structure; it was only in the later years that
they noticed that these gifts were at war with the
excessive irritability of his nerves. Josef August
Röckel (the tenor who sang Florestan in *Fidelio*),
who saw a good deal of him from 1806 onwards, tells
us in his reminiscences that Beethoven " seemed
marked out for a Methuselah, and it must have been
a maleficent influence of unusual might that could
bring this strong column to ruin so much before its
time." In 1810, when, at the age of forty, his constitution was probably already undermined, his deafness had become incurable, and he was fast developing into a hypochondriac, he gave Bettina Brentano
the impression, when she met him for the first time,

of being no more than thirty. Schindler is at pains to combat the tendency of the artists to depict Beethoven as the weary Titan whose head was bowed under the weight of his own and the world's sufferings; none of his contemporaries, he says, ever knew him to carry his head in any way but proudly erect, even in his hours of physical ill-being. As he lay dead his friends were impressed, as Goethe's were on a similar occasion, by the magnificence of his torso.

In his first years of fame in Vienna his too exuberant strength and confidence in himself found partial expression in a pride of bearing that many people found objectionable, and in a rudeness of manner that was not wholly the result of his upbringing in Bonn, but of a deliberate intention to make his weight felt. He seems to have had no doubt from the commencement that he was at least the equal of Mozart and Haydn; and he soon made himself unpopular in Viennese musical circles by his undisguised contempt for the majority of his rivals and the caustic terms in which he expressed his opinion of them. Czerny describes him as discussing other musicians and their music, past and present, "with the greatest positiveness and with pointed and often caustic wit, and always from the lofty standpoint assigned him by his genius and from which he looked out upon art, with the consequence that his judgments even of the classics were mostly strict, and full of the consciousness of his own equality with them." Elsewhere Czerny tells us that " his verdicts on other men's music were always right, but — especially in his younger years — very sharp, biting, and lacking in consideration." Griesinger, the Saxon ambassador in Vienna, said that " many people shook their heads at that time and called the young Beethoven arrogant and immoderately proud." His pupil Ferdinand Ries tells us that each of Beethoven's three teachers in Vienna (Haydn, Albrechtsberger, and Salieri) said of him that he was " so obstinate and self-willed that there was much he would have to learn through hard experience." Haydn's good-humoured nickname for him was " The Great Mogul."

Many of his own utterances during these early years bear unconscious witness to this proud sense of his own strength. His remark, in one of his letters, that he valued people only for what he could get out of them must not be interpreted in any narrow sense. A more generous, altruistic artist than Beethoven has perhaps never existed; and this remark of his was merely the expression of an over vitalized young spirit eager to use the whole world to promote the spiritual development of which it felt itself capable. So again were his remark that " Power is the morality of men who are above the common, and it is mine," and his assurance to his friends, after Jena, that if he understood the art of war as he did that of music he would give Napoleon a beating. These and other dicta of the kind, some naïve in their arrogance, some a little unpleasant on the surface, were merely the superb strength of the man seeking an outlet for itself. A Greek dramatist would have seen in his later history the gods' punishment of his *Hubris*. The gods may perhaps have handled him more wisely than we know, and our sympathy with his misfortunes may, after all, be a trifle misplaced. It is significant that in the documents he has left us bearing upon his deafness, what he bewails is not its possible influence upon him as a composer but its frustration of all his impulses to realize himself in outward action. He would by now have gone over half Europe, he says, as a piano virtuoso; and there is little reason to doubt that he would have received an important Kapellmeister's post somewhere or other and had a great deal of his energies fritted away in official duties.

The desire to impress himself upon the world and to see the flattering evidence of the impression with his own eyes is evident through all the negotiations for a visit to London: he knew his high place in the world and his extraordinary power over men. We can only speculate, of course, as to what his life would have been if his deafness and his other bodily ills had not chained him to Vienna, made the career of a public performer impossible for him, and driven him more and more in upon himself; but there is fair

warrant for believing that the forced concentration
of his mighty physical and mental vitality upon
composition alone was a blessing in disguise for
him. *

VI

As he grew older his arrogance and self-suffi-
ciency became less noticeable in matters of music,
but took the curious form of the most unwarrantable
interference with the lives of his relations, beginning
with his two brothers and ending with his nephew
Carl; and accompanying this interference, and probably at the root of it, was a hatred of their women-
folk that passed the bounds of reason.

Johann had become an apothecary in Linz. (He
subsequently made a fortune by supplying the
French army with medicaments.) His house there
being too large for him, he rented part of it to a
physician from Vienna, with whom there came to
live, besides his wife, the latter's sister, Thérèse
Obermayer. Johann fell in love with Thérèse, and
the girl became his mistress. The news of this
brought the composer in hot haste to Linz in 1812,
the principal object of his journey being, as Thayer
says, simply " to interfere in Johann's domestic affairs." He overbearingly insisted that his brother
— a man of thirty-five, and perfectly independent
of him — should break off the connection. " Excited
by opposition," says Thayer, " Ludwig resorted to
any and every means to accomplish his purpose. He

saw the Bishop about it. He applied to the civil authorities. He pushed the affair so earnestly as at last
to obtain an order to the police to remove the girl to
Vienna if, on a certain day, she should still be found
in Linz. The disgrace to the poor girl; the strong
liking which Johann had for her; his natural morti-
fication at not being allowed to be master in his own
house; these and other similar causes wrought him
up almost to desperation." What added the last
straw to his resentment seems to have been one of
those outbursts of vile temper and scurrilous language which we know, from his letters and the reminiscences of friends, to have been all too frequent
with Beethoven. Johann decisively settled the matter by marrying Thérèse, and Ludwig "lost the
game and immediately hurried away to Vienna,
angry and mortified that the measures he had taken
had led to the very result which he wished to pre-
vent; had given to the unchaste girl the legal right
to call him 'brother'; and had put it in Johann's
power — should he in the future have cause to rue
his wedding-day — to reproach him as the author
of his misfortune. Indeed, when that unhappy future came, Johann always declared that Ludwig
had driven him into the marriage."

Thérèse turned out to be a rather worthless character, whose infidelities were notorious. Beethoven
was forever urging Johann to get rid of her, and at
one time the latter thought of doing this, though

he afterwards deemed it wiser to make no public
trouble but to retain his wife at any rate as a house-
keeper, in which capacity she shone. Ludwig and
Carl went to stay with Johann at Gneixendorff in
the autumn of 1826; it was on his return to Vienna,
at the end of the year, that the composer caught the
chill that was the beginning of his fatal illness. During the visit he showed, in exaggerated form, his im-
placable hostility to Johann's wife, speaking to her
as little as possible, and trying to induce Johann to
disinherit her and leave the whole of his fortune to
Carl. It says something for the tolerance of the
woman that in spite of all this she should have attended him during his fatal illness; indeed, by the
irony of fate, she and Anselm Hüttenbrenner were
the only two people with him when he died.

Brother Caspar was no more fortunate in the matter of the virtue of *his* wife: it was Ludwig's disap-
proval of her morally that made him fight as he did
to oust her from the guardianship of her son. While
giving him all credit for his basic unselfishness in
this affair and for his profound love for the boy, we
can hardly admit that he was fully justified in his
conduct of the campaign against the widow, or even
that his actions were always those of a quite sane
man. It is unpleasant to read of his persistent attempts to prejudice Carl against his mother, and of
his encouragement of the boy to think and speak ill
of her. At the root of it all, it can hardly be doubted,

was a perverse sex-obsession. We have a curious
sidelight on this in his dealings with the village
priest Fröhlich, who had to dismiss the boy from his
school because he feared he would have a bad influence on the other scholars, Beethoven having " en-
couraged his nephew to revile his mother, applaud-
ing him when he applied vile epithets to her," and,
as Fröhlich testified to the court, " the boy had confessed to me that while he knew that he was doing
wrong he yet defamed his mother to curry favour
with his uncle, and dared not tell him the truth because he would only believe lies." Carl's conduct in
general did not commend itself either to the school
authorities or to the inhabitants of the village, and
there was nothing for it but for the priest to dismiss
him from the school. Thereupon Fröhlich in his turn
became the victim of Beethoven's morbid sex-complex; in a letter to the Magistracy he asserted that
the priest " is despised by his congregation," and
" suspected of being guilty of illicit intercourse."
" The association of these men [i.e., the priest and
the government clerk Hotschevar, who acted as the
widow's advocate and was afterwards appointed
one of Carl's guardians] with Madame van Beethoven *bears witness* against them both, and *only
such* could make *common* cause with Madame van
Beethoven *against me*." (Italics in the original.)

VII

POSTERITY has too readily taken these and similar outbursts of Beethoven at their face value. It is hardly surprising, perhaps, that a man who was always so ready to give himself the handsomest testimonials for moral perfection should be, in large part, taken at his own estimate; but the most elementary sense of justice ought to have suggested to some of the more pious biographers that there are two sides to every case, and that a man's denigration of other people is not to be accepted without question merely because he happens to have written some of the world's greatest music. Putting aside the theory of deliberate misrepresentation on his part, there is always the possibility of his having been ill-informed, or over-hasty in his assumptions, or over-credulous towards tale-bearers, or even in the last resort not quite sane, in the full sense of the word, on this one matter. To this last point we shall have to recur later; meanwhile it is necessary to say frankly that it is time the more obsequious biographers ceased to construct a super-moral Beethoven out of their own inner consciousness and drew him as the evidence shows him to have been. No biographer could have a profounder sense of the greatness of his subject than Thayer had of his; but Thayer had a judicial habit of mind that is all too rare among the biographers of great composers, and he found it impossible either to conceal or manipulate the facts (except in one pardonable instance, with which I shall deal later), or to burke the conclusions that naturally emerged from the facts. The conception of Beethoven as a man of almost impeccable goodness and a moral loftiness hardly attainable by the ordinary individual found no favour with Thayer: his patient researches had given him too much first-hand knowledge of the subject.

Let me say, at the outset, that Beethoven himself quite innocently helped to make the legend that has encased him almost impenetrably for three or four generations. It will be my thesis that he neither posed nor consciously deceived, but simply that in his life, as in his music, he was the unconscious expression of forces profounder than the merely volitional. He did not do wrong things knowing they were wrong, and then try to persuade the world that there was no wrong in them. The truer explanation is that, partly by reason of his overwhelming belief in himself, partly because of his almost complete failure to understand the world in which he lived what most people would call his real life, but which was actually only a dim shadow-world trailing along behind the inner musical world that was the sole true reality for him, he was incapable of seeing certain of his actions as other people saw them. A typical case is that of his dealings with the publishers in the matter of the Mass in D. The summing up may be given in the sober words of the impartial Thayer: —

"It is now desirable to disregard the strict chronological sequence of incident and dispose, so far as is possible, of the history of the great Mass in D prior to the adoption of a new plan by which Beethoven hoped to make it a source of extraordinary revenue. So far as it affects Beethoven's character as a man not always scrupulous in his observance of business obligations, the story does not need to extend beyond the year 1822. Careful readers of this biography can easily recall a number of lapses from high ideals of candour and justice in his treatment of his friends and of a nice sense of honour and honesty in his dealings with his publishers; but at no time have these blemishes been so numerous or so patent as they are in his negotiations for the publication of the *Missa Solennis* — a circumstance which is thrown into a particularly strong light by the frequency and vehemence of his protestations of moral rectitude in the letters which have risen like ghosts to accuse him, and by the strange paradox that the period is one in which his artistic thoughts and imagination dwelt in the highest regions to which they ever soared. He was never louder in his protestations of business morality than when he was promising the Mass to four or more publishers practically at the same time, and giving it to none of them; never more apparently frank than when he was making ignoble use of a gentleman, whom he himself described as one of the best friends on earth, as an intermediary between himself and another friend to whom he was bound by business ties and childhood associations which challenged confidence; never more obsequious (for even this word must now be used in describing his attitude toward Franz Brentano) than after he had secured a loan from that friend in the nature of an advance on a contract which he never carried out; never more apparently sincere than when he told one publisher (after he had promised the Mass to another) that he should be particularly sorry if he were unable to give the Mass into his hands; never more forcefully and indignantly honest in appearance than when he informed still another publisher that the second had importuned him for the Mass ('bombarded' was the word), but that he had never even deigned to answer his letters. But even this is far from compassing the indictment; the counts are not even complete when it is added that in a letter he states that the publisher whom he had told it would have been a source of sorrow not to favour had never even been contemplated amongst those who might receive the Mass; that he permitted the friend to whom he first promised the score to tie up some of his capital for a year and more so that 'good Beethoven' should not have to wait a day for his money; that after promising the Mass to the third publisher he sought to create the impression that it was not the *Missa Solennis* that had been bargained for, but one of two Masses which he had in hand. It is not only proper, but a duty, to give all possible weight to the circumstances which can be, ought to be, must indeed be pleaded in extenuation of his conduct; but the facts cannot be obscured or ignored without distorting the picture of the man Beethoven as this biography has consistently striven from the beginning to present it."

The devil's advocate, indeed, could make the most damagingly malicious play with the long story of Beethoven's dealings with publishers and producers. Years before he wove such embarrassing entanglements about himself in the matter of the Mass in D his peculiar views on business morality had got him into very evil odour in London. Ries, "with much trouble," had in 1815 persuaded the London Philharmonic Society to order three overtures from Beethoven. "Imagine," says Thayer, "the disappointment of these men, i.e., the distinguished musicians composing the Society, fresh from the performance of the C minor Symphony, when they played through the overtures to *The Ruins of Athens* and *King Stephen*. . . . Nor was the *Namensfeier* thought worthy of its author." Ries tells us that of the three works sent, " not one of them, in view of Beethoven's great name and the character of these concerts, could be performed, because expectation was tense and more than the ordinary was asked of Beethoven. A few years later he published all three,[1] and the Society did not think it worth while to complain. Amongst them was the overture to *The Ruins of Athens*, which I consider unworthy of him." " But when," to continue Thayer's comments, " it became known that neither of the three — op. 115 possibly excepted — was new, and that not one of them had been composed to meet the Society's order, is it surprising that this act of Beethoven was deemed unworthy of him, disrespectful, nay, an insult to the Society, and resented accordingly? "

Beethoven followed up this achievement with certain dealings with the publisher Birchall that can hardly be regarded as ideally " straight," with the result that the London publishers seem to have come to the conclusion that he was scarcely a person

---

[1] Which was a breach of his agreement of 5th February, 1816, by which he bound himself, in consideration of the payment of seventy-five guineas, not to allow the orchestral score and parts to be published without the Society's permission, and reserved the right of performance and the further right to issue them in pianoforte arrangements *after* they had been performed in London.

with whom further business relations ought to be cultivated. " For God's sake, don't buy anything of Beethoven! " was a passage in a letter sent to Charles Neate (Beethoven's London intermediary) after the trial of the overtures; while Neate's attempts to sell the works in London were met with an " utter refusal in all quarters." " He besought Mr. Birchall to purchase the overtures. The reply was : ' I would not print them if you would give me them gratis.' "

VIII

BUT it is more particularly in matters of sexual
morality that Beethoven has succeeded in creating
around himself a legend that does not correspond
with the reality. The biographers cite approvingly
his dismissal of a slut of a maidservant because she
did not rise to the lofty level of his own idea of
chastity; and his hatred of the unchaste wives of his
two brothers has been counted unto him for right-
eousness. But though Beethoven's music has probably fewer sex-connotations than that of any other
composer except Bach's, there can be no question
that as regards women he was a normally consti-
tuted male. His pæans upon chastity amount to no
more, in the last resort, than do the certificates he
so lavishly bestowed upon himself for his exceptional scrupulousness in business matters. In his
youth and early manhood he had been a good deal
of a lady-killer. Already in the years immediately
succeeding his death the legend seems to have been
gaining currency that, as befitted the composer of
the Ninth Symphony, the last quartets, and the
Mass in D, Beethoven had always been above the
more obvious frailties of the flesh; and it was probably to correct this growing legend that his friends

Wegeler and Ries assured the readers of their reminiscences that so far from Beethoven never having been in love, he was practically never out of it, and indeed generally in it very seriously: " he made several conquests," says Wegeler, " that would have been, if not impossible, at all events very difficult even for an Adonis." He was very fond of pretty women, says Ries, and " when we passed a fairly charming girl in the street he would turn round, study her closely through his eye-glasses, and laugh or grin when he saw I had noticed him. He was frequently in love, but mostly only for a short while each time. Once when I teased him about the conquest of a certain lovely lady he confessed that she had held him captive longer and closer than any of the others — a full seven months." " Never," says Ries a little later, " did he visit me oftener than when I lodged with a tailor who had three pretty but quite irreproachable daughters."

In the later years of his life he managed to give his acquaintances and callers the impression of being a man above the weaknesses of sex. His friend Friedrich Wähner expatiates on the " wonderful consistency " of the inner and the outer man in Beethoven as in other " exceptional beings." To-day we know that two beings more completely dissimilar than Beethoven the composer and Beethoven the man could hardly be found. Wähner comes no nearer the truth when he says that " as regards his moral character we can say of him that he now and then was overcome by affections, but never by passions "; and that " just as he withstood like a man the temptations of wine, so he seems never to have been seduced by the power of love," which we know to be nonsense. We know the names of several of the objects of his passion. Dr. Bertolini, who was his friend and physician from 1806–1816, tells us that he generally had a " flame," and that in addition he was also given to flirtations " from which he did not always emerge happily "; (*daneben* " *miselte* " *er auch gewöhnlich, wobei er nicht immer gut wegkam*).[1] Yet though his copious amoristic life was well enough known to his close associates, a casual acquaintance like Dr. Aloys Weissenbach, who met him in 1814, and who has left some reminiscences of him that are remarkable for their penetrating observation, could take away with him the impression that " he is so hot on moral rectitude that he can no longer be friendly with anyone in whom he has once perceived a moral taint. . . . In the matter of the sin of sensuality [*in Hinsicht auf die Sünde der Lust*] he is unspotted; he could repeat Bürger's *Lied von der Manneskraft* to all the men of Vienna."

---

[1] " *Miseln*," says Kerst (*Die Erinnerungen an Beethoven*, II, 193) = " *liebeln*, an expression that Goethe also used to employ in his letters to Frau von Stein." (The editor of the 1848 edition of *Goethe's Briefe an Frau von Stein* has the following note to a letter of the poet's of 1776, " Aus der Terminologie der damaligen geistreichen Gesellschaft: misel, schöne; miseln, schön thun.")

Thayer's summary of this passage and his comment upon it are significant: " Remarks [by Weissenbach] follow upon Beethoven's ignorance of the value of money, of the absolute purity of his morals (which, unfortunately, is not true), and of the irregularity of his life."

IX

THE words " which unfortunately is not true," coming from Thayer, are significant. Thayer was the last man in the world to wish to dwell upon the failings of Beethoven; when he permits himself a reference to them it is with no malicious desire to reduce the great composer to the ordinary level of mankind, but purely and simply from a conviction that the biographer's duty is to speak the truth and nothing but the truth. Speaking the whole truth is a different matter: in one case only did Thayer not feel called upon to do that, and we can understand his reticence. But as a certain amount of evidence in connection with the subject has gradually leaked out, and it is a matter of common knowledge that Thayer had in his possession evidence which he could not bring himself to make public, it is impossible now for the writer upon Beethoven to attempt to avoid the subject. It is even desirable that it shall be discussed freely and soberly, for, in the first place, a plain statement of the facts is the surest way to put an end to rumours and speculation that go beyond the facts, and in the second place no student of Beethoven as man and artist can doubt the importance of the matter in his life.

This generation does not approach, or, it would be more correct to say, evade the subject of venereal disease with the prudery of the generation or two immediately preceding. With greater social frankness on the subject has come a welcome tendency to put moral judgments on one side and to see it mainly as a question of hygiene, individual and social. No apology, then, need be made at this time of day for an inquiry, free from the bias imported by moralic acid, into the question of the syphilis from which Beethoven is said to have suffered. So long as the question is burked, so long will the field be open to the amateur, theoretician and the social moralist with all sorts of bees in his bonnet.[1] And the only proper way to approach the question, in the case of Beethoven, is that of the scientist or the physician, to whom a venereal disease is not a matter for moralizing but simply one disease among

---

[1] The type is to be seen in perfection in a recent book by Brunold Springer, *Die genialen Syphilitiker*. No one is safe from Springer. Setting out from the comprehensive assumption that, as he puts it, " civilization is syphilization," he explains in terms of this disease the lives and thoughts and actions of a large number of representative men, from Pope Alexander VI in the fifteenth century and Leo X in the sixteenth through Ulrich von Hütten and Benvenuto Cellini and Mirabeau and Napoleon and E. T. A. Hoffmann and Beethoven and Heine and Schopenhauer and Schumann and Manet and Maupassant and Daudet and Nietzsche and Hugo Wolf and many others, down to Woodrow Wilson and Mussolini. It is impossible to separate fact from conjecture in Springer's book, which reveals an obsession and a habit of mind that may easily become a social danger, for no one is more notoriously incapable of weighing evidence than the moralist riding his pet hobby-horse.

others. Beethoven's supposititious syphilis, if it is to be discussed at all, must be discussed with the same freedom from moralic prepossessions as his early smallpox or his later typhus. And the only justification for discussing the question at all is that it may possibly throw some light on the mind and the conduct of Beethoven.

For about half a century it has been known — or confidently assumed — that some time in his early manhood Beethoven had contracted syphilis, and the further confident assumption was made that this was the ultimate cause of his deafness. This was the view taken by Sir George Grove, who, in his article on Beethoven in the first edition of the *Dictionary of Music and Musicians* (1879), after detailing the results of the *post mortem* examination of the auditory apparatus, said that " the whole of these appearances are most probably the result of syphilitic affections at an early period of his life," and he adds in a footnote, " this diagnosis, which I owe to the kindness of my friend Dr. Lauder Brunton, is confirmed by the existence of two prescriptions, of which, since this passage in the text was written, I have been told by Mr. Thayer, who heard of them from Dr. Bartolini " (*sic*). It has been a matter of common knowledge for some time that Thayer had evidence on the subject that he did not think it advisable to publish, and there can be little doubt that his main source of information was Bertolini, who was Beethoven's friend and physician for ten years or so from 1806 onwards.[1] " Through a caprice of Beethoven," says Thayer, " his cordial relations with Dr. Bertolini came to an abrupt end about 1815; but the doctor, though pained and mortified, retained his respect and veneration for his former friend to the last. In 1831 [four years after the composer's death] he gave a singular proof of his delicate regard for Beethoven's reputation; supposing himself to be at the point of death from cholera, and being too feeble to examine his large collection of the composer's letters and notes to him, he ordered them all to be burned, because a few were not of a nature to be risked in careless hands."

Within the last few years a searching examination of the whole of the available evidence in the matter of Beethoven's deafness has been made by a German physician, Dr. Waldemar Schweisheimer,[2] who comes to the conclusion that the deafness can be fully accounted for by the typhus from which the composer is said to have suffered at one time (typhus was endemic in Vienna in that epoch), and by the digestive and related troubles that plagued Beethoven all his life. He sees no reason to assume syphilis as a cause, and demands proof that Beethoven ever suffered from that disease. He may or

[1] He was a pupil and assistant of another of Beethoven's physicians, Dr. Malfatti.

[2] *Beethovens Leiden, ihr Einfluss auf sein Leben und Schaffen*, Munich, 1922.

may not be right [1] as regards the causation of the deafness, but he shows something less than ideal scientific objectivity in his treatment of the other question.

Schweisheimer's argument really amounts to nothing more than a contention that we should decline to place any reliance on the alleged " evidence " until it is published. That line of reasoning would be valid enough in most cases, but it has to be remarked that the evidence has been withheld in the case of Beethoven not because of any desire to secure, as it were, a conviction by suppressing vital facts, but because of an exceptional and commendable feeling of piety towards the great composer. The question of the weight to be attached to this " evidence " is not a specifically medical one, as Schweisheimer would make out; it is a question simply of common sense. Thayer's carefully chosen words with regard to Bertolini are decisive. It is perhaps not surprising that from the wording of one portion of Thayer's statement a number of people have been led to assume that Bertolini died about 1831. This was not so, however. He lived till long after the middle of the nineteenth century, and Thayer knew him personally. We have only to read Thayer's sentences with a perfectly open mind to

---

[1] An opposite view is taken by another German medical man, Dr. Leo Jacobsohn, in the *Deutsche Medizinische Wochenschrift*, No. 36, 1910, and in *Der Tag*, 12th December, 1919.

realize that Bertolini had given him confidential information about Beethoven's disease, and, indeed, shown him his own prescriptions in the case — the prescriptions referred to by Grove. Why should a medical man, believing himself to be at the point of death, be so concerned about leaving behind him evidence that Beethoven suffered from anything so exempt from conventional moral reproach as typhus? Thayer expressly speaks of Bertolini's " delicate regard for Beethoven's reputation "; but how could his or any other composer's " reputation " be involved in any revelation as to his having had typhus in his early manhood? The documents — letters and notes — were destroyed by Bertolini lest they should fall into " careless hands." Once more, if the documents did not reveal a malady that had not merely physical but moral connotations — which cannot be said of typhus or deafness — could their falling into the most careless hands imaginable do the slightest harm to Beethoven's " reputation " ?

As late as 1912, Theodor von Frimmel, the well-known Beethoven researcher, wrote, in a study of Beethoven's deafness, that in addition to possible predisposing causes such as measles and scarlatina there was " another " that might be assumed, " about which I must not keep silence, since many years ago Thayer gave me, by letter, definite information about this *other* malady of Beethoven's."

And Dr. Jacobsohn follows this up by saying, "After Frimmel's communication I do not feel I am committing any indiscretion when I say that in the private possession of a man of culture [*Gelehrter*] in Berlin there is an as yet unpublished note in Beethoven's own hand referring to a cure that leaves no doubt as to the specific nature of his malady."[1]

While we can understand, then, Dr. Schweisheimer's desire[2] to shield Beethoven from the imputation of having contracted syphilis in his youth, we cannot give any weight to his insistence that we ought to reject Thayer's and the other evidence until the documents are published. They have been withheld from publication merely because of the unsavouriness of the subject, and out of "piety" towards Beethoven's memory. A biographer of Thayer's exceptionally judicial habit of mind would not have said all he did say on such a matter unless he had been absolutely sure of his facts.

In his chapter dealing with the composer's personality he permits himself a further veiled reference to the topic in a discussion of "Beethoven's

---

[1] André de Hevesy, in his *Beethoven: Vie Intime* (1926) says that in a memorandum in Beethoven's writing of the year 1819 the composer notes that he must get " L. V. Legunan, *L'Art de connaître et de guérir toutes les contagions vénériennes.*"

[2] A desire which, it may be noted in passing, contrasts oddly with his own previous dictum that to the physician a disease is simply a disease, the moral or social implications of a particular disease not coming into consideration.

moral principles." " Spending his whole life," he says, " in a state of society in which the vow of celibacy was by no means a vow of chastity; in which the parentage of a cardinal's or archbishop's children was neither a secret nor a disgrace; in which the illegitimate offspring of princes and magnates were proud of their descent and formed upon it well-grounded hopes of advancement and success in life; in which the moderate gratification of the sexual was no more discountenanced than the satisfying of any other natural appetite — it is nonsense to suppose that, under such circumstances, Beethoven could have puritanic scruples on that point. Those who have had occasion and opportunity to ascertain the facts, know that he had not, and are also aware that he did not always escape the common penalities of transgressing the laws of strict purity."

X

THE fact of Beethoven's malady seems then to be beyond dispute, and the knowledge of it helps us, perhaps, to a better understanding of his conduct in certain junctures. It would account for his venomous hatred of notoriously unchaste women, and for his desire to protect his brothers from them. As early as 1796 we find him writing from Prague to his brother Johann, who had just come to Vienna, warning him of the dangers of the capital: "I hope your residence in Vienna will please you more and more — only beware of the whole tribe of bad women." The knowledge that his own life had been radically changed for the worse by a youthful imprudence would make him anxious to save the younger members of his family from a similar misfortune. He did not, it is true, surrender his own right still to fall in love as often as he chose; but his disease made him, as a similar disease did Schopenhauer, an insensate hater of women whose sensuality was their most notable characteristic. And we have here the explanation of a good deal of his conduct towards his nephew Carl. He saw the beloved boy exposed, as he thought, to a double risk — his own too lively temperament, and the influence of a mother whose morals were not what they might have been. His excessive restrictions upon the goings and the comings, the companions and the amusements of his nephew, and his occasional brutality towards him, all become more intelligible in the light of his own sexual history; he probably had an agonized vision of the pleasure-loving and easily-led Carl coming to moral and physical shipwreck in the stews of Vienna. And, as we have seen, the morbid sex-complex revealed itself in other ways, as in his reckless aspersions of the sexual morality of the village priest the moment the latter crossed his wishes in the matter of Carl.

His own conduct in the affair of his nephew is hardly consistent at all points with normal sanity, and this seems to have been the view taken of it by most of his contemporaries — especially the courts — who did not, as posterity can hardly help doing, allow their sense of plain justice to be corrupted by admiration for him as a composer. His taking possession of Carl was in the first place a breach of a solemn trust. Carl Caspar (the father) was under no illusions about his wife, but he thought enough of her, and had small enough faith in the general capacity of his brother, to be unwilling that the latter should have the boy's destiny wholly in his own hands as he desired. The dying man saw the impending danger, and made, to the best of his ability, express provision against it in his final testament. The codicil to his will runs thus: —

" Having observed that my brother, Herr Ludwig van Beethoven, desires after my death to take wholly to himself my son Carl, and wholly to remove him from the supervision and bringing-up of his mother, and moreover, seeing that the best of concord does not exist between my brother and my wife, I have found it necessary to add to my will that I absolutely do not wish that my son Carl be taken away from his mother, but that always, in so far as his future career shall permit, he shall remain with his mother, to which end she as well as my brother are to exercise the guardianship of my son.[1] Only by concord can the object be obtained which I had in view in appointing my brother guardian of my son; wherefore, for the well-being of my child, I recommend *compliance* [*Nachgiebigkeit, pliancy*] to my wife, and more *moderation* to my brother, God permit them to be in concord for the good of my child. This is the last wish of the dying husband and brother. Vienna, November 14, 1815."[2]

---

[1] How history has been falsified on this point may be judged from a single typical instance: Lenz, in his *Beethoven et ses trois styles,* told his readers that " His brother [Caspar] had by will made him the guardian of his son, but the mother would not relinquish the guardianship to her brother-in-law."

[2] Carl Caspar died two days later.

Ludwig's first act, after his brother's death, was to " declare his suspicions that the end had been hastened by poison! " — another of the many acts of his that indicate what a social peril a good man can be if his actions and his tongue are not controlled by normal common sense.[1] His second act was to take legal steps to exclude the widow from the guardianship, on the ground of her old-time infidelity. In this he succeeded, though his success was only the prelude to a long warfare with the widow, conducted both in the courts and out of them.

Thayer has stripped, as he puts it, " the story of the quarrel between her and her brother-in-law of the romantic excrescences " that gradually became fastened upon it by the more uncritical biographers. Beethoven's morbid sex-obsession made it utterly impossible for him to do the widow the most elementary justice, even to the extent of believing her disinterestedly affectionate in wishing to see her own child occasionally. His own unfitness for the duties of guardian he could never be brought to recognize; still less could he see the evil influence he was unconsciously exerting upon the boy in some respects. An ageing hypochondriac, a bachelor, completely unused to children, almost stone deaf, living alone in surroundings that were not remarkable either for their comfort or their cleanliness, was

---

[1] He would not be convinced until Bertolini, upon his insistence, had made a *post mortem* examination.

hardly the best guardian conceivable for a lively boy. His obvious unfitness for the task, in spite of his honourable intentions, was dwelt upon by the widow's advocate, Jacob Hotschevar, in his petition to the *Landrecht* on her behalf. The boy was alleged to be not only in a fair way to become morally perverted but was sadly neglected physically: " his feet and hands are frozen,[1] he has no winter clothing; he seems to be whole weeks without a change of linen; for a pocket-handkerchief a sheet of blotting-paper often has to serve, and as Herr Ludwig van Beethoven is unmarried, little thought appears to be given to the general cleanliness of his linen and his person." The boy had been quick to see that in order to keep in favour with his uncle he must at least pretend to be of the latter's way of thinking, especially as regarded his mother. " He is . . . a hypocrite: he declares that he is compelled to lie and dissemble, because his guardian will not believe him when he speaks the truth; he must always speak otherwise than as he thinks, or as the facts are." Hotschevar again and again pays generous tribute to Beethoven's lofty intentions, but insists that in spite of these the boy is suffering morally and physically from his exclusive association with his uncle.

---

[1] It was the winter of 1818. The documents, which are only summarized in the American edition, are given in full in the German edition of Thayer (Appendix III to Volume IV).

Carl's own testimony before the court goes far to bear out the advocate's contentions: one cannot read to-day without a pang of pity the little fellow's statement that " he would like to live at his uncle's if only he had a companion, as his uncle was almost deaf, and he could not talk to him." The courts in general were plainly on the side of the widow, in spite — or perhaps because — of the fact that to one of them the composer addressed a letter in which, as Thayer says, he " proclaimed the magnanimity and virtuousness of all his acts, and discharged a broadside of accusation and insinuation against Madame van Beethoven and the priest who had come to her help." As usual, he recklessly flung unsupported charges against the widow, even alleging that she " gave him [Carl] money to awaken in him lusts and desires which are harmful." In 1819 the court, after a patient examination of all the facts of the case, declared that " the boy had been subject to the whims of Beethoven and had been tossed back and forth like a ball from one educational institution to another," and made an order that the mother, " the natural guardian under the law," was to have charge of the boy, with " an honest and capable man " (Leopold Nüssbock) as co-guardian in place of Beethoven. The further history of the dispute cannot be given in detail here: it must suffice to say that it was not until 1820 that a higher court set aside the judgment of the lower, and appointed

Beethoven and Councillor Peters as co-guardians of the boy, the mother being excluded.[1]

---

[1] The document in which the lower court justifies its findings deals very severely with Beethoven. It censures his " unproven chatter " about the character of the widow, and his obviously fanatical and inappeasable enmity towards her. The higher court, perhaps, was not uninfluenced by the fact that Beethoven was known to be the protégé of the Archduke Rudolph.

XI

W E have only to dissociate in our minds the Beethoven we see in this affair from the Beethoven who wrote the nine symphonies to see that the former was in many respects anything but a normally rational man. From his childhood he seems to have moved about in a mental world of his own, circumscribed for him both by the limitations of his intelligence (apart from music) and by the defects of his upbringing. Even as a boy his real mental life was lived in an inner world of music, the outer universe being only a puzzling shadow-world that irritated him by its refusal to work along the lines of the other. Bernhard Maurer, who, with some thirteen years' seniority, was his colleague in the Bonn Court Kapelle, tells us that in 1780 the ten-year-old Beethoven made the acquaintance of Zambona, who noted that "outside music he knew nothing pertaining to social life, and that consequently he was moody with other people, did not know how to take part in a conversation, and kept to himself, so that he was looked upon as a misanthrope" — at the age of ten! Zambona took the boy's neglected education in hand, and besides teaching him the customary rudiments, imparted to him some knowledge of Latin. His notoriously bad manners in the early Vienna years were no doubt in part a defiant attempt of the plebeian to assert himself against his aristocratic patrons by an obstinate insistence on the most obvious points of difference between them — on the principle of one of the characters in Mr. Shaw's play, who advises another never to admit a fault, but to make a virtue of it; in part also to sheer inability to take his bearings properly. The adoring nineteenth century biographers were wont to exult over some of his exhibitions of ill-breeding, which they read as evidences of a noble democratic spirit — the celebrated affair, for instance, in which Goethe figured, with the Imperial family. But Beethoven, while refusing to pay deference to others, had a very strong sense of the deference due to himself. Unwilling to treat his aristocratic friends with ordinary courtesy, he insisted on the utmost respect being paid by them to him. At a supper given by " an old Countess " in honour of Prince Louis Ferdinand he greatly resented not being given a seat at the Prince's table; " he flew into a rage, made a few ugly remarks, took his hat, and went away." His contempt for orders and decorations and diplomas when possessed by others was not inconsistent with a willingness to go in quest of them for himself; and his pride in the gold medal, weighing twenty-one Louis d'or, that was given him by the King of France, was so great that his friends had difficulty in persuading him not to wear it in public. Though the London Philharmonic Society had commissioned the Ninth Symphony from him, he asked the publishers to hold back the printed score until he had had time to send a manuscript copy to the King of Prussia, to whom the work was dedicated. " He wanted," says Thayer, " an Order, and had he received one in time for the concert, its insignia would, in great likelihood, have graced his breast on that occasion. He had repeatedly expressed contempt for the outward signs of royal condescension, but the medal sent by the King of France had evidently caused a change of heart in this regard. He was eager to see a description and illustration of the medallion in the newspapers; and that he thought of hanging it about his neck appears from a remark to him made by Carl before the concert, telling him that it was too heavy to wear and would pull down his collar."

On the surface it seems as if the disparity between the man and the artist was no less great in the case of Beethoven than in that of Wagner. Thayer found it difficult to reconcile the exalted spiritual mood in which he wrote the Mass in D with the lapses from ordinary honesty in his dealings with the publishers over the Mass. His conduct in the matter of Carl and his mother it is impossible to reconcile at times with the most elementary notions of fair dealing. As we have just seen, he was angrily, contemptuously critical of " honours " that happened to come other men's way, yet by no means unwilling that they should come his, and, while priding himself on his rudeness to his aristocratic friends and patrons, up in arms at the most trifling fancied slight to himself. His letters overflow with expressions of love for his fellow men, of which there is not the slightest reason to doubt the complete sincerity; yet his normal attitude towards them, it is hardly too much to say, was one of almost insane suspicion; whoever differed from him was a liar, a thief, an adulterer, a poisoner. His repentances were generally as swift and as complete as his offences, but the number and the intensity of the offences is hardly consistent with ordinary sanity. The truth seems to be that he had no sense of the realities of the world in which he was compelled to live his bodily life. The only real world for him was that of music; it puzzled and fretted him that the world that other men called real did not proceed upon the same lofty and simple principles as that other. Once he had made the painful discovery that the two were not the same he sank into the hypochondria and the misanthropy that were the wonder and the distress of all who knew and loved him. His pupil Ries, who knew him probably as well as any man did, tells us that each of his three teachers in Vienna — Haydn, Albrechtsberger and Salieri — had said that Beethoven was " so obstinate and self-willed that he would have to learn many a thing by hard experience that he could not bear to take instruction upon." The hard — cruelly hard — experience came in due time. In all that concerned his art he was able to make it his own; in all that concerned life he can hardly be said to have been any wiser than he was at the beginning. Here he could assimilate nothing; the most he could do was to let his hypochondria grow upon him, and to shut himself up more and more from a world he could not understand.

Of his inability to round off his corners and fit more or less comfortably into the scheme of ordinary life we have testimony enough. Along with his great strength went a pathetic clumsiness in all things, physical no less than mental. " In his behaviour," says Ries, " he was very awkward and maladroit; there was a total lack of grace about his clumsy movements. He could rarely take anything in his hands without letting it fall or smashing it. He would often knock his inkstand into his piano, which stood by his writing-desk. No furniture was safe when he was near it — least of all if it was valuable; everything was knocked over, dirtied and broken. It is a mystery how he managed to shave himself, so many were the cuts on his face. He could never learn to dance in time." Of his absent-mindedness many stories are told — how he would at one time leave a restaurant without paying, while at another he would call for his bill without having eaten anything; and how his friends, reduced to despair at the condition of his clothes and linen, would remove the offending garments while he was asleep, and replace them by others, without his observing the change. He had an instinct for the grander things in literature, things built on his own heroic scale; but it is difficult to see in him any signs of real critical judgment. The pseudo-religious, pseudo-metaphysical sentences from Oriental and other moral literature that he would copy out and have framed and keep before him on his desk are merely sonorous platitudes. His humour generally took the form either of clumsy punning or of horseplay. Some of the stories told of him suggest a mental structure that in other men we should be inclined to describe as stupidity. A humorous friend having written him from Berlin that the latest invention there was a lantern for the blind, Beethoven took the story in all seriousness, passed it on to his friends in Vienna, and was furious when it was broken to him that he had been hoaxed. The simplest arithmetical calculation was almost beyond him. " There are pitiful proofs in the Conversation Books," says Thayer, " that simple sums in addition were more than he could master," and there are few more pathetic pictures in the whole history of music than that of the great composer, during his last illness, struggling, under the tuition of his nephew, with the elements of multiplication. The

Conversation Book for the 4th, 5th and 6th December, 1826, contains simple sums set him by Carl, with explanations: "Multiplication," the boy writes, "is a simplified form of addition, wherefore examples are performed in the same manner. Each product is set under its proper place. If it consists of two digits, the left one is added to the product of the next. Here is a small illustration: 2348 multiplied by 2."

He can really be said to have lived, in the true sense of the term, only in his moments of " raptus " —the word by which Frau von Breuning characterized, in the early Bonn days, his absorption in his musical dreams; and the emergence from this raptus was often as painful, both for himself and his associates, as the return of a somnambulist or hypnotized dreamer to ordinary consciousness. Several of his friends have described the harrowing effect of his loud, harsh laughter on occasions such as these. Julius Benedict told Thayer: "When I first saw him in Baden, with his white hair, that streamed down over his powerful shoulders, his knitting of the brows when anything specially moved him, and his prodigious laughter, that was indescribably painful for the hearer, I was as moved as if King Lear or one of the old Celtic bards were standing before me." Marie von Breuning was told by her mother that "his lively gesticulations, his loud voice and his reckless conduct towards others startled people in the street, and often she felt ashamed because they stopped and took him to be crazy. His laughter was especially loud and extraordinarily shrill."

In social intercourse, as in his art, he would suddenly make the most unexpected transition of mood, but without harmonizing the transition as he so well knew how to do in music. "Last year," he told Schnyder, "I was improvising on the piano before a small company, when all at once I saw that the fools were weeping. I ran away, and played no more to them." Cherubini called him an unlicked bear. More than one acquaintance likened him, in his misanthropy, to Rousseau. Baron de Trémont, who met him in 1809, said, "He shared with Rousseau certain erroneous opinions that had their origin in the fact that the misanthropic temper of each of them created for him a world of fantasy that had no relation to human nature and to the social state." "His character," said Czerny, "was very like that of Rousseau, but his disposition was noble, big-hearted and pure." Goethe said that Beethoven found the world "detestable," adding, "but he does not thereby make the world any more enjoyable either for himself or others." Zelter, in 1819, wrote of him, "He is intolerably *maussaude*: some people say he is an idiot. That is easily said: God forgive us all our trespasses! The poor man is completely deaf." That he was a privileged mad genius, not accountable for his actions in ordinary life, seems to have been the opinion of the Vienna police. Wilhelm Christian Müller tells us that the composer was given, in the restaurants, to airing loudly and satirically his opinions on all subjects, especially the Government, the police, and the ways of the great. " The police knew all about it, but left him alone, either because they thought him a fantast or out of consideration for his brilliant genius as an artist " — or sometimes, we may conjecture, because of his well-known association with the Archduke Rudolph, the half-brother of the Emperor Franz.

XII

IN his life, as in his art, we are perpetually intrigued by the question of how differently he might have developed had his deafness never descended on him. It is too often forgotten that — notwithstanding Maurer's description of him as a misanthrope at the ripe age of ten — there is little or nothing in the picture we have of him as a young man to lead us to suppose that he was predestined either to misanthropy or what, for want of a better word, we may call mysticism. Ignaz von Seyfried, who was in close association with him from 1800 to 1806, living in the same house and seeing him almost daily for a long period, tells us that Beethoven " was at that time cheerful, ready for any fun, jovial, sprightly, full of the joy of life, facetious, often satirical; as yet no physical malady had seized upon him; his days were not clouded by the loss of a sense that is peculiarly indispensable to the musician; there had only remained to him weak eyes as an after-effect of smallpox in his early childhood." As a young man he was evidently cheerful enough so long as the puzzling outer world did not press too closely upon him. Thayer is right in saying, à propos of the years 1807 to 1809, " A popular conception of Beethoven's character, namely, that a predisposition to gloom and melancholy formed its basis, appears to the present writer to be a mistake. The question is not what he became in later years — *tempora mutantur, nos et mutamur in illis* — but what was the normal constitution of his mind in this regard. Exaggerated reports of his sadness and infelicity during the last third of his life became current even before its close, and prepared the public to give undue importance to the melancholy letters and papers of earlier years, which from time to time were exhumed and published. The reader, upon examination, will be surprised to find how few in number they are, at what wide intervals they were written, and how easy it is to account for their tone." Thayer seems justified in tracing, in part, the Heiligenstadt "Testament" of 1802 to one of those momentary fits of depression that come upon every artist in the exhaustion that follows a period of intense cerebration. The young Beethoven was too tough to remain depressed for long: and we must agree with Thayer that "notwithstanding . . . the occasional characteristic complaints in his letters," the three years 1807, 1808 and 1809 " were unquestionably the happiest in the last half of his life."

But from about his fortieth year the clouds began to close down upon him. His deafness increased; his disease, barring him, the most affectionately domestic of men, from marriage, must have been, apart from its physical distress, a sore trial to his spirit; and the more he came into contact with the realities of life the more difficult he found it to harmonize them with his inner world. There came a period of bitter hypochondria, then one of a hypochondria melancholy and resigned, from which there welled a pathetic sweetness that sometimes racked the hearts of those who knew him. The unshakable strength of the man and his power to abstract himself from the outer world and live in a dream-world of his own saved him from the despair that would have been the ruin of most other artists in his position. Even in his defeats he remained heroic. It was characteristic of him that in his moments of greatest suffering, though he made the conventional verbal play with the conventional consolations of religion, it was to the antique pagan world that he went to renew his spirit's strength. " I have often cursed my existence," he wrote to Wegeler in 1801; and adds immediately, " *Plutarch taught me resignation.*" His hero and his model was Brutus. He could not understand the present and the world of little men about him; he was a lofty, lonely mountain peak that looked across the valleys towards its mighty peers.

Even the bitterness died out of his hypochondria as he retired more and more within himself, giving up as hopeless the attempt to reconcile the world within him and the world without. We have a number of moving records of the profound impression he made on friends and visitors in his latter years. The inappeasable spiritual hunger of the unhappy man could be read in his eyes. It was the melancholy expression of these that struck the young Swedish poet Atterbom, who saw him during the winter of 1818/19. "The man," he wrote, "is of short stature, but strongly built; he has profoundly thoughtful, melancholy eyes, and a face in which not a trace of joy in life can be perceived." Rochlitz's impression of him in 1822 was that of "a man of a rich, eager spirit, of an unfettered, never-resting imagination; a man . . . thrown as it were on a desert island, where he had meditated and brooded upon his experiences till fragments came to seem the whole to him, fancies became convictions, which he confidently and confidingly cried to the world." Blahetka, writing to Schindler in 1840, recalled him as a man "who from his own standpoint was bound to judge entirely falsely everything around him, since he had within himself no criterion for right judgment, and, confined to his own world of ideas, had never learned to step out of himself. He was probably more or less fully conscious of this himself, wherefore he always sought among his associates for intermediaries between himself and the world, and it was precisely these intermediaries who almost invariably abused him. How completely his idealism overrode his power of judgment is evident from almost every step he took in ordinary life. He simply could not understand that things and the relations of things were in reality different from what he conceived them to be; and so it was very difficult, in the long run, to be in close association with him without friction."

On Johann Sporschil, in 1823, he made the impression, as he had done on Benedict, of "one of Ossian's grey-haired bards of Ullin." [1] To Rellstab, in 1825, he seemed exhausted and out of tune; nevertheless there was in his face "nothing of the harshness, the tempestuous breaking of restraint, that people lend to his physiognomy in order to bring it into agreement with his works. . . . Sadness, suffering, and goodness I could read in his face; but, I repeat, not a trace of asperity, of the tremendous hardiness that characterizes the flights of his spirit. I would not deceive the reader with an invention of my own; I would give him only the truth, be only a faithful mirror of a dear image. Notwithstanding all I have said, he lacked nothing of the mysteriously attractive power that draws us so irresistibly to the outward appearance of great men. The sorrow, the dumb and heavy grief that were expressed in his face were not the result of the indisposition of the moment — for I always found the same expression during the following weeks, in which

[1] In English in the original.

Beethoven's health was much better — but the effect of his whole life's experience, in which the highest assurance of realization had been blended with the cruelest ordeal of denial. And so the spectacle of this silent and profound affliction, visible in his sorrow-laden brow, in his gentle eyes, affected me more than I can describe. It needed the utmost self-control to sit face to face with him and keep back one's tears."

In these last years, indeed, what moved his visitors most deeply was the melancholy sweetness in the face of the mortally wounded old lion, and the unexpected gentleness of his manner. Within himself he had attained to a spiritual transfiguration, and in moments when life ceased to draw its puzzling zigzags across his simple spirit something of the inner light shone through the rugged, fissured rock that was the outer man. The music of this period, too, melts every now and then into a touching gentleness and sweetness and wistfulness. We see it in little things like his new use of the " feminine ending." These endings are at all periods comparatively rare in Beethoven, and when they do occur they are either from the octave to the seventh, from the third to the second, or from the sixth to the fifth; moreover they come more often in the course of a phrase than as a final cadence. The feminine ending of a descent from the fourth to the third — the softest and tenderest of all — and at the conclu-

sion of a melody, as in the slow movement of the E
major piano sonata (Op. 109) : —

is an exceeding rarity in his music. The correspond-
ingly expressive droop in the minor is from the third
to the second, and it is this progression that gives its
pathetic wistfulness to the second part of the melody of the Arietta in the last piano sonata (in C
minor, Op. 111) : —

This melting beauty is not often found in Beethoven's music; indeed, in such a passage as this from

the first variation upon the above-quoted theme of
the andante from Op. 109: —

we seem to be in the full flood of the later roman-
ticism. In a weaker spirit this mood would have de-
generated into a self-pitying beating of the breast;
with Beethoven it is like an infinitely tender caress
from a giant's hand. And at no other period of his
life, and in no other mood, would he have ended a
big work with the passage shown in No. 1, as it were
a sigh of regret dying away upon the night air. Truly
in his art, if to a less extent in his life, he had
learned, as his earliest Vienna mentors said he
would have to do, from sad experience. " Out of the
eater came forth meat: and out of the strong came
forth sweetness."

PART II
THE COMPOSER

I

THIS conception of Beethoven the man as an instrument used by the spirit of music to realize itself through, rather than as a normal being who, during certain intervals in his bodily existence, wrote music, is confirmed when we observe the unconscious workings of his mind. It could be shown, I think, that all composers' minds are more or less unconscious mechanisms. To some extent, indeed, this must be true of all artists: even prose writers will be found, on examination, to have each his own peculiar rhythm. But for some reason or other connected no doubt with the nature of the material in which the musician works, the composer is specially given to the unconscious repetition of the same formulæ. That these have so far not been noticed and isolated except in a few of the most obvious cases, such as Gounod's sequences or Grieg's falling thirds, is one of the mysteries of music; for if any poet or prosaist were to employ the same verbal formula as many thousand times as the composer employs the same musical formula we should find him unreadable.[1] Beethoven's slow movements show

---

[1] I hope to demonstrate, in a later book, this unconscious tyranny of the formula over the musician's imagination, illustrating it from the works

him to be obsessed by a certain little figure from his earliest days to his latest — a figure of three ascending notes in conjunct motion, that generally come in about the same place relatively to the melodic design as a whole, and are unconsciously used to perform the same expressive function.[1]

These three ascending notes are to be seen in the adagio of his first piano sonata (Op. 2, No. 1), in the passage marked A in the following quotation: —

No. 4

of a number of composers. One strange feature of the case is that though there are only twelve notes in the scale, no two composers have what I would call the same finger-print. Even the least mistakable of them all — the sequence — is a different thing with a Wagner and with a Gounod. Another odd feature of the case is that while we may be immersed all our life in a composer's music and never become aware of the half-dozen or so finger-prints that make his individual style what it is, once we become, by accident, conscious of them and begin to look for them, we find them written on almost every page of his music.

[1] It goes without saying that this figure will be found in other men's music; that is inevitable, seeing the limited number of notes that form the octave. What makes this or any other phrase a "finger-print" of a particular composer, however, is the fact that in no other composer's music will it be found to recur so persistently, and always at relatively the same point and with the same purpose. If I see a man eating three oranges at dinner one day, I must not draw at once the inference that he is overwhelmingly fond of oranges. But if, after observing him at dinner every day for a year, I find that he invariably eats three oranges and no other fruit, I am entitled to draw the conclusion that oranges have a special attraction for him.

They will be found again, towards the end of his
life, at the climactic point of the slow movement of
the Ninth Symphony (finished in 1823) : —

Were No. 4 A an isolated experience, we might regard the fragment as merely a portion of a conventional melodic stride, such as might be made by any
composer on his way to a salient accented note of
his phrase. But its recurrence in the adagio of the
Ninth Symphony is of itself enough to set us thinking, for there, obviously, the fragment is not a piece
of conventional filling-in, but is of the utmost importance to Beethoven's idea. We might, at a pinch,
eliminate it from No. 4, substituting for it another
E, or a C, or a rest, or anything else we liked that
would serve as a diving-board for the plunge into
the F of the next bar. But no such procedure would
be possible in the case of the example from the
Ninth Symphony. There the three notes are not a
mere leaping-off point but a vital part of the musical idea; take them away, or substitute any other
notes for them, and Beethoven is prevented from
saying what he intended to say. And in the light of
this fact we begin to suspect that in the case of the
quotation from the first piano sonata also the frag-

ment, though rather more conventional, being part
of a melody that has not the vitality of that in the
Ninth Symphony, fulfils the same intellectual function.

We are confirmed in this opinion first of all when
we see Beethoven using it again, this time in a less
debatable way, in a later stage of the melody, and,
secondly, when we find him making use of it in hun-
dreds of other places in his music. The melody that
begins as No. 4 is developed later thus : —

No. 6

The G in the second bar is merely an appoggiatura;
essentially the progression is D, E, F; and here the
fragment has something of the emotional urgency
and inevitability of its equivalent in the Ninth
Symphony; we could not substitute any other notes
for these, as, in a moment of scepticism, we might
do for No. 4 A.

In the largo of the second piano sonata (Op. 2,
No. 2), we find the fragment again in various forms.
Sometimes, as in the eighth bar, it is merely a device
of transition from the opening melody in D major
to a contrasting one in A major. But we meet unmistakably with the obsession of the three ascending notes in various other parts of the movement.

The opening phrase presents us with it slightly disguised by the rhythm : —

while a little later we meet with it again twice in an
inner part (also in the bass) : —

the melody heaving itself up to its climax in the
same way and at relatively the same point as that
of the Ninth Symphony does. If it be thought that
this tracing of the three notes in this passage is a
trifle far-fetched, examination of the same method
of procedure in other slow movements of Beethoven
— especially the Cavatina of the B flat quartet (Op.
130) — will dispose of the objection. The three-
notes obsession frequently showed itself in the inner
or the lower as well as in the highest melodic part.
We will consider this aspect of the case later. Meanwhile, proof that the inner part of No. 8 is a fruit
of the three-notes obsession may be had in the fact
that when the melody is repeated in full (after the
momentary excursion into A major to which reference has been made above) the same inner part becomes, with a slight modification, the climax of the
melody itself : —

No. 9

Here the basic principle of the three-notes sequence undergoes a certain expansion, as occasionally happens elsewhere in Beethoven's melodies at the climactic point — in the following passage, for example, from the adagio of the third piano sonata (Op. 2, No. 3) : —

No. 10

In the largo of the fourth sonata (in E flat, Op. 7), the swelling to a climax by means of the three notes is unmistakable : —

No. 11

while a little later they are used repetitively, in a way not infrequent with Beethoven, to intensify the impression of climbing to a height : —

No. 12

In the adagio of the fifth sonata (in C minor, Op. 10, No. 1) the main melody, as sometimes happens with Beethoven (though rarely in the slow movements that aim at intensity of expression) proceeds on other lines than those I have indicated, the obsession of the three notes not declaring itself till a supplement to the chief theme comes: —

This, as the reader will recognize, is a foretaste of the *Pathétique* (the eighth sonata, Op. 13). In the preamble to this latter, Beethoven is more passionately serious than in any of his preceding works, and accordingly the upward-striving figure of three notes dominates the whole musical idea; the phrase: —

is repeated, in one form or another, no less than ten times in the eleven bars that constitute the slow introduction to the allegro; and by this time it is impossible to doubt that the figure was inwrought into the very tissue of Beethoven's thinking in those moods in which he set himself to write his slow movements.

We find it again, of course, in the adagio of the *Pathétique* (twice): —

Let us resume the examination of the sonatas in chronological order. The sixth has no slow movement. The theme of the largo of the seventh sonata (in D major, Op. 10, No. 3) : —

No. 16

introduces the three notes explicitly at the end of our quotation, while they are implicit twice in what has gone before.

The ninth sonata has no slow movement. In that of the tenth (in G major, Op. 14, No. 2), there is no escaping the typical fragment, either in the opening phases : —

No. 17

or in their continuation, where we have something of the same kind of intensification by repetition as in example No. 12 and in the introduction to the *Pathétique:* —

No. 18

In the opening melody of the adagio of the eleventh sonata (in B flat, Op. 22), we have an instance of the disguising of the three-notes progression by means of chromatics and appoggiature: —

No.19

while in the later stages we see the *Pathétique-Tristan* spirit again at work, using the now familiar figure as its medium: —

No. 20

In the theme of the *andante con variazioni* of the twelfth sonata (Op. 26), the sequence of the three notes is broken, as we have seen happen in other cases, by an appoggiatura: —

No. 21

Later comes the premonition of *Tristan* once more:

No. 22

In the opening andante of the thirteenth sonata (*sonata quasi una fantasia*, in E flat, Op. 27, No. 1), the upward surge is prolonged: —

No. 23

while the adagio shows the figure in various forms: —

No. 24

including the typically Beethovenian use of it in an
inner part: —

No. 25

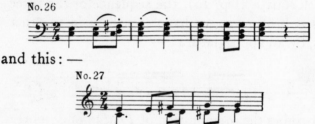

a mood and a procedure that are familiar to us from
such passages as this from the allegretto of the
Seventh Symphony: —

No. 26

and this: —

No. 27

in the latter of which we have another case of the
prolongation and intensification of the figure in the
inner part by a chromatic note.

The procedure in the andante of the fifteenth
sonata (Op. 28) is the same as in examples No. 8,
No. 26, No. 27 and other cases: —

No. 28

In the adagio of the sixteenth sonata (in G major,
Op. 31, No. 1), the three notes are used to manœu-

vre the theme to its peak, as in No. 5 and elsewhere: —

No. 29

while in the adagio of the seventeenth sonata (in D
minor, Op. 31, No. 2), in addition to the threefold
repetition of the figure in the melody: —

No. 30

we find it again in the inner and lower parts at the
climax: —

No. 31

and later it is repeated sequentially: —

No. 32

In the eighteenth sonata (in E flat, Op. 31, No. 3)
a modified form of the figure is used to arrest our
attention in the opening bars of the first allegro: —

No. 33

It may not be amiss to remind the reader once more that while this particular sequence of three notes is bound to occur somewhere or other in almost any piece of music, what makes it a Beethoven finger-print is its invariable use for the same purpose of emotional expression at very much the same point. While the employment of it for this purpose is not absolutely restricted to the slow movements, its occurrence in rapid movements is rare. The first subject of the *Waldstein* sonata (No. 21, Op. 53) looks on the surface like a utilization of the figure for an allegro movement, but the phrase, though consisting, in essence, of three ascending notes, has not quite the distinguishing marks of the examples already cited — the creation of a feeling of uplift, or tension, or emotional intensification, at a climactic point in the melody. It may well be that the obsession had an occasional overflow, as it were, into other than slow movements, and the opening subject of the *Waldstein* is probably a case of this kind. There is more of the meaning that the figure carries in the examples quoted above in the later transitional passage to the second subject of the *Waldstein*: —

No. 34

where the conjunct ascending notes are undoubtedly employed to create the impression of working

up to something. The three-notes figure is used in
the customary Beethovenian way in the adagio of
the *Waldstein:* —

No. 35

again in the four-bars preamble, in slow time, to
the allegro of the twenty-fourth sonata (in F sharp
major, Op. 78) : —

No. 36

and again in the *Lebewohl* section of the twenty-
sixth sonata (in E flat, Op. 81a) : —

No. 37

where the quasi-moral upward urge is manifest.
And how closely the figure was associated in Beethoven's mind with this feeling of uplift or of tension may be estimated from its absence from the
slow movements of virtually unbroken placidity,
such as that of the twenty-seventh sonata (in E
minor, Op. 90), or of such an andante as that of the
Appassionata, that consists, so far as thematic material goes, only of sixteen bars of majestic evenness
(with a great leap near the end), the remainder being a series of variations.

H

The figure was not a mere tag to which Beethoven was subject at one particular period of his life. It runs through all his work. Whenever he opened the floodgates of feeling, the obsession asserted itself; and the more profound the emotion, as in the slow movements of the latest works, the more certain we are to find the figure being impressed into service, and made to carry a heavier weight of meaning than in any of the earlier works. Thus in the very expressive adagio of the twenty-eighth sonata (in A major, Op. 101) the familiar figure becomes the medium for one of Beethoven's most moving utterances: —

No. 38

(The harmonies are quoted only in the bars containing the figure.)

In the *Hammerklavier* sonata (the twenty-ninth, Op. 106) the figure is used twice in the opening phrase of the adagio: —

No. 39

while in the andante of the thirtieth sonata (in E
major, Op. 109) we have what is in essence the
usual figure, but this time made more intense by
the abandonment of the conjunct motion at one
point : —

No. 40

In the thirty-first sonata (in A flat, Op. 110), we
have a hint of it in the opening phrase : —

No. 41

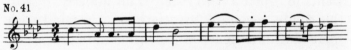

In the wonderful arietta of the last sonata of all, the
thirty-second (in C minor, Op. 111), the figure is
seen, in the first half of the theme, in an inner part
in the third bar and in the melody in the eighth bar,
in addition to four uses of it in the bass (not shown
in our quotation) : —

No. 42

and in the second half it conducts the theme to its
climax of uplift in the customary way (see example
No. 2).

Compare with this the use of the figure in Beethoven's song *Die Ehre Gottes aus der Natur*, where we have the words to give us a clue to what was in his mind: —

No. 43

und laüft den　Weg　gleich als　ein　Held

Not, be it understood, that he has a hero in mind each time he employs this figure, but that when he wants to depict a hero rising in his majesty, it is to this figure, generally associated in his mind with some indefinite image of expansion, intensification, or soaring, that he spontaneously reverts.

II

THIS use of the figure of three notes in the slow movements is by no means confined to the piano works. There is, in fact, no genre cultivated by Beethoven in which it is not to be found. It appears several times in the adagio of the first Piano Trio (Op. 1, No. 1) : —

No. 44

(Harmonies added here in the sixth bar only. Note the veiled use of the figure in the fourth bar.) Too much stress need not be laid on its tentative appearance in the third bar of this quotation, but there is no mistaking its significance in the sixth bar; the family resemblance between this figure and that in the quotation from the Ninth Symphony is beyond question. In the largo of the second Piano Trio (Op. 1, No. 2), again, while the figure as it first appears in the main theme carries no special significance with it, it is made to carry the usual meaning later : —

No. 45

The theme of the andante of the String Trio in E
flat (Op. 3), is, curiously enough, constructed
wholly of repetitions of this figure; but it is only
when we come to the climax that we feel that it
affiliates to the other examples quoted: —

No. 46

though the very liberal employment of it throughout
the andante shows how easily, from his earliest
years, Beethoven fell under the spell of this obsession as soon as he sat down to write a slow movement; even when it expresses nothing in particular
he cannot get away from it. It is undoubtedly meant
by the young Beethoven, however, to carry a great
deal of expression in the adagio of the String Trio
(Serenade) in D major (Op. 8): —

No. 47

a phrase that brings up in our mind the theme of
the funeral march in the *Eroica* of several years
later: —

No. 48

There are hints of the figure in the rather negligible slow movements of the String Trios in G major (Op. 9, No. 1) and D major (Op. 9, No. 2) and C minor (Op. 9, No. 3). In the last of these, Beethoven's marking of *adagio con espressione* shows how much in earnest he was; and though we of to-day cannot find very much that is " expressive " in the movement, the mere seriousness of intention on the composer's part at once brings the obsession into play: —

No. 49

We meet with it again in the *adagio con espressione* of the Piano Trio in B flat (Op. 11): —

No. 50

It is impossible here to pursue the figure through each of Beethoven's chamber works; it must suffice to draw attention to a few of the more notable uses of it. It is especially sure of being found when Beethoven is aiming at intensity of expression, as in the *adagio affetuoso ed appassionato* of the F major quartet (Op. 18, No 1) : —

No. 51

and the *adagio cantabile* of the Septet (Op. 20) : —

No. 52

The theme of the *adagio molto espressivo* of the Quintet in C major (Op. 29) commences with a three-fold statement of the figure: —

No. 53

After having made its appearance in the opening bar of the theme of the andante of the C major Quartet (Op. 59, No. 3), it takes almost complete possession of the later stages of the theme, not only in the upper but in the lower parts: —

No. 54

In the great Piano Trio in B flat (Op. 97), two preparatory employments of it lead up, in the fifth bar, to one of Beethoven's weightiest uses of it: —

No. 55

In his last years, as we have seen in the case of the piano sonatas and the Ninth Symphony, the obsession was so deeply rooted in him that he came more and more to rely on it in moments of deep feeling. It figures several times in the brief adagio introduction to the B flat Quartet (Op. 130), not only in the opening phrase : —

No. 56

but in the supplement to this : —

No. 57

The full extent of the obsession, however, is seen in the noble and moving Cavatina from this quartet, which Beethoven has marked *adagio molto espressiva*. The following quotation in score of the first fifteen bars will show how irresistibly the figure kept recurring in Beethoven's consciousness when he was in his most emotional mood : —

No. 58 Adagio molto espressivo

In the first violin the figure occurs in the 2nd, 4th, 5th/6th, 11th, 13th/14th and 15th bars; in the viola, in bars 9/10, 12/13; in the cello, in bars 1, 2, 3/4, 7, 8/9, 9/10, 11, 13/14.

We meet with it again, at the climactic point, in the supplement to the main melody: —

No. 59

while it is an essential part of the famous *beklemmt* interlude that follows this: —

No. 60

The Cavatina contains in all only sixty-six bars; the three-notes figure occurs, in the various parts, no less than forty-two times, the two extreme parts, the first violin and the cellos, significantly having it most often.

Attention need be drawn to only a few of the most striking examples of the use of the figure in other works of Beethoven. We find it freely employed at critical moments in the slow movement of the Fifth Symphony, when the music begins, as it were, to summon up its energies for combat and victory: —

No. 61

Even in a quasi- " slow movement " from which passion is absent, such as that of the Eighth Symphony (the marking is *allegretto scherzando,* but the movement fills the place in the symphonic scheme usually occupied by an andante), Beethoven cannot escape the obsession when he comes to the climax of the melody: —

No. 62

We meet with it in the opening phrase of the larghetto of the Second Symphony: —

No. 63

which seems to anticipate the *Prometheus* overture: —

No. 64

while the chromatic use of the figure in bars 4 and 5 of the last quotation correlates, on the one side with the Second Symphony: —

No. 65

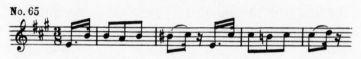

and on the other side with the Ninth: —

No. 66

It is put to energetic use in the *Leonora No. 1* overture: —

No. 67

and again, this time in a quieter mood, in the *Leonora No 3:* —

No. 68

It is the essence both of the typical *Egmont* theme: —

No. 69 Sostenuto

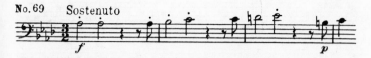

and of some later expansions of this: —

No. 70

We find it in the *maestoso e sustenuto* introduction
to the *weihe des Hauses* overture: —

No. 71

Again in the largo of the first piano concerto, much
disguised, however, by added notes: —

No. 72

in the largo of the third piano concerto: —

No. 73

and later in the same movement: —

No. 74

and a remarkable quadruple use of it in the adagio
of the fifth piano concerto: —

No. 75

Examples of it can be culled by the hundred from
the songs: here only two or three can be quoted:
From the *Busslied:* —

No. 76 Poco Adagio

An dir al-lein, an dir hab' ich ge-sün-digt,

and again: —

No. 77

und mei - ne Thrä nen sind vor___ dir__

From *Bitten*: —

No. 78 Religioso

Gott, dei - ne Gü - te reicht so weit, so

weit die Wol - ken ge - hen

From *Liebes-Ungeduld*: —

No. 79 Andante con espressione

So muss ich ihm ent-sa - gen, dem Lang' ge-nähr-ten

Hof-fen, und meiner Sehnsucht Klagen ver-hallen still in Schmerz

From *Gretels Warnung*: —

No. 80

Das merkt' er, ach _ und liess nicht nach, bis

er es all, bis er es all, bis er es all _ er hielt

From *Nimm sie hin:* —

und   du singst, und du— singst, was ich ge-sun-gen,

From *Kriegslied der Oesterreicher:* —

Ein gro-sses deutsches Volk sind wir, sind mächtig und ge-recht.

From *Sehnsucht:* —

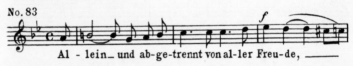

Al - lein— und ab-ge-trennt von al-ler Freu-de, ____

From *Die Ehre Gottes aus der Natur* (already quoted as No. 43).

From the violin sonatas the following examples may be selected: From Op. 12, No. 2: —

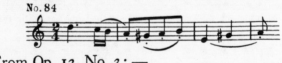

From Op. 12, No. 3: —

From Op. 96: —

From the *Kreutzer:* —

No. 87

and: —

No. 88

From the Mass in D: —

No. 89

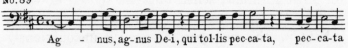

Ag — nus, ag-nus De-i, qui tol-lis pec-ca-ta, pec-ca-ta

From the *Leonora Overture No 3:* —

No. 90 Adagio

and: —

No. 91

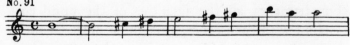

I

III

Examples enough have been given, I think, to show the reality of this obsession of Beethoven's. That some of them have no particular expressive significance is a further proof of the persistence of the little formula; when once he settled down to write a slow movement he could hardly escape from it. But for the most part he used it unconsciously as the culminating point in the expression of a musical idea that had associations of uplift, of tension, of yearning towards a height, of soaring resolution. Not, of course, that he would ever formulate to himself any such verbal equivalents of the idea. But the musical imagination does not work in a watertight compartment; all the faculties of the mind correspond with each other, and much more frequent than the cases of deliberate pictorial or poetic imitation in music are the cases in which the composer's musical idea has been influenced by an external association that lies too deep down in his subconsciousness for even himself to be aware of it.

The persistence of this three-notes figure through the whole of Beethoven's enormous output seems to indicate that almost every one of his slow movements came from much the same fundamental mood; it is hardly too much to say, indeed, that they are just so many attempts to fix in sound one haunting vision. Two points are worthy of note in this connection. First, that, in the main, Beethoven's slow movements do not show his mind at his greatest. Perhaps a dozen or so of them do; the others often seem like sketches for their mightier fellows. He found himself much earlier in his allegros than in his andantes; several of the first movements in the early chamber works unmistakably reveal the coming giant, while the slow movements are often feeble. Second, at no stage of his career does he show anything like the same imaginative variety and technical resource in his slow movements as in his fast ones. In the latter he is forever creating new worlds, as a simple comparison of the first movements of the nine symphonies, the chamber music works, and the concertos will show. His slow movements have a marked family likeness of mood, while he seemed to the very end to have difficulty in developing this mood musically as he so easily could the others.

There may possibly have been historical as well as personal reasons for this limitation of resource; it may be that only after the romantic movement had set free a large fund of emotion did the extended slow movement become possible. Certain it is that the construction of a slow movement on the same symphonic scale as the other movements, the steady working out of a highly charged emotional state at great length, as in such slow movements as those of Brahms's and Elgar's first symphonies, was something Beethoven never attained to. His favourite manner of extending the original idea was by means of variations. Sometimes the results were strangely trivial — again an indication that he was not as completely at home in this kind of movement as in the faster ones. The variation method became more and more firmly fixed in him as he grew older; and in some of his latest and greatest slow movements he draws the most magical expression from his variations. Where he did not adopt this plan he cut the movement relatively short; as we have seen, the Cavatina in the B flat quartet — one of the profoundest of his utterances — which retains the song style throughout, extends to no more than sixty-six bars. In the A major piano sonata (Op. 101) he writes one of his most moving adagios — "full of longing," he has marked it; but as the general design of the sonata apparently did not permit him to treat it in variation form, it remains a mere matter of twenty bars. The extended adagios of three of the last four piano sonatas (in the other he is content with a recitative and a short lament in song form) all proceed by way of variation, as does also the adagio of the Ninth Symphony. The method in this last is virtually the same as in the Fifth

Symphony: the original outline of the melody is subjected to smaller and smaller indentations. When we observe the new problems he had posed for himself in the other movements of the Ninth Symphony, and the variety of imagination and of technical device he brought to bear upon the solution of them, the persistence of the old variation method in the adagio of the Ninth Symphony is all the more remarkable.

It all leads to the conclusion that in the vein for which the slow movement is the recognized form of expression the greater Beethoven had comparatively little to say; his andantes and adagios, indeed, may, with a little licence, be described as a long attempt to free himself from one particular emotional complex. The persistence of the figure of three notes in these movements is only one of the factors in this conclusion. That obsession is perhaps the most remarkable of the many features of Beethoven's style that tempt us to think of him as the unconscious medium through which a musical idea worked, rather than as the conscious discoverer and manipulator of the idea. But here again we must beware of being led astray by words. No one would contend that either Beethoven or any other composer has been a merely passive mouthpiece through which some undiscoverable spirit spoke. The processes of the human soul are too subtle and too complex to be described in this rough-and-ready way. But everyone whose daily business is with literature or art knows that nowhere in the whole domain of human psychology is the old problem of free will and predestination more baffling than here. Undoubtedly we shape, or fancy we shape, our ideas into the forms we desire; but as undoubtedly the ideas have a life of their own. It is a common experience for a writer, after having given a projected article a certain title and developed his subject, as he thinks, along the line he intended when he began, to find, after he has proceeded a little way, that the article has taken quite another line. This is not due to slackness of attention, to mere wandering of thought; it proceeds from the fact that at some point or other a section of the original idea has developed a life of its own in the subconscious, and has from that point onwards taken control of affairs unknown to the writer. If the divagation were due to mere failure of cohesion in the thinking, the article would not hang together at the end as it does. The truth is that another, a subconscious, line of logic has substituted itself for the line that the writer thought conscious and under his control; and all that he has to do ultimately is to accept the new situation. He began by writing out a title and intending to develop the subject suggested by it; he ends by having another subject subconsciously developed for him, and nothing remains to be done but to cross out the original title and write in another.

These subconscious or unconscious processes go on in all artists; but Beethoven seems to have been exceptionally under the control of them.

IV

'IT is his paradox that he, seemingly the freest of
instrumental composers, the richest in invention,
the most fertile in technical devices for the realization of his idea, should be the one who can most
clearly be seen at almost every point to be obeying
a voice of which he was unconscious, but whose
commands were imperative. It is astonishing to
what a small number of formulæ — melodic, rhythmic, and so on — his apparently so varied procedure
can be reduced. Points of this kind were not perceived by the earliest students of Beethoven, who,
like Schindler and Lenz, were more conscious of the
æsthetic and intellectual differences between his
" three styles " than of the basic formal and technical unity of them. Their strong sense, indeed, of the
mental and moral growth of Beethoven as an artist
from his first period to his second, and from his second to his third, actually stood in the way of their
perceiving how like, in a great many respects, the
final Beethoven was to the earliest. From one point
of view Lenz is shrewdly right when, contrasting
Mozart with Beethoven, he says that in the case of
the former, if we look at his work over a long period

of years we see that it is the artist who has progressed, while the man is the same, whereas in the case of Beethoven we see that not only the artist but the man has developed with the years. But the perception of this fact must not blind us to another — that from the beginning to the end of his career Beethoven was unconsciously occupied in realizing the same fundamental impulses, and realizing them along basically the same technical lines.

His melodic style has been most searchingly analysed by Dr. Hans Gál,[1] who shows him to have unconsciously gravitated more and more towards a type of melody that Gál calls " absolute," by which he means purely diatonic melody without suspensions on the strong beat — " the old Celto-Germanic folk melody," in fact. The antithesis to this type of melody is the Mozartian, the distinguishing marks of which are "the plentiful use of suspensions [retardations], of ornaments growing out of these, and of chromatics." A perfect example of that style is the andante of Mozart's G minor symphony. Beethoven's melody has more affiliations with Haydn's than with Mozart's, and so far from Beethoven having "grown out of" Mozart in this respect, the truth is that as he developed he unconsciously shook off the first Mozartian influence upon him and

---

[1] In an article entitled *Die Stileigenthümlichkeiten des jungen Beethoven*, in the *Studien zur Musikwissenschaft* issued in conjunction with the *Denkmäler der Tonkunst in Oesterreich* (Viertes Heft, 1916).

settled more and more into his natural vein of "absolute melody." As Gál says, in his younger days Beethoven would almost certainly not have harmonized the first theme of the fourth piano concerto as he has done. In the second bar of the theme the first and fifth quavers, and in the third bar the first crotchet, are what Gál calls "latent retardations"; as a very young man Beethoven would probably have treated these notes quite frankly as retardations, and harmonized them accordingly; whereas the Beethoven of 1805 treats the notes as independent and gives them harmonies of their own. Gál contends that had the youthful Beethoven been harmonizing the E major aria in *Fidelio*: —

he would have treated the last bar somewhat after the Mozartian fashion: —

whereas what the mature Beethoven does is to har-

monize all the notes out, as he did in the case of the
theme of the fourth piano concerto: —

No. 94

It was the unconscious bias towards " absolute melody " that made him dispense more and more with
retardations as he grew older.

We have seen how persistently the little figure of
three notes occupied Beethoven's mind in his slow
movements. This, however, though his most curious
and — when once we become aware of it — most
obvious obsession is not his only one. By a more
copious use of music type than is possible here it
would be easy to show how the same basic idea
keeps cropping up again and again in works of different periods, and, on the surface, different characters. The theme of the andante of the Fifth Symphony, for example: —

No. 95

which, it will be remembered, appears in its first
form in the Sketch Book thus: —

No. 96

obviously reappears at the commencement of the
Leonora No. 3: —

No. 97

One can hardly doubt that it is the same noble ges-
ture in each case: a similar mood in Beethoven has
evoked a similar phrase. But if anyone should question this, there can be no question whatever as to
the brotherhood of the following themes: —

From the sextet for strings and two horns, Op.
81b. (in spite of the opus number this is an early
work, dating from 1794/5): —

No. 98

From the wind sextet, Op. 71 (1796/8): —

No. 99

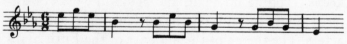

From the septet (1800): —

No. 100

From the B flat concerto (1795): —

No. 101

From the sonata for horn and piano (1800) : —

No. 102

As Gál says when quoting these passages, " how great is the distance between these and the mighty, precipitously falling main theme of the first movement of the Ninth Symphony : —

No. 103

yet the latter has sprung from the same ground-idea."

Many other unconscious " moments " of Beethoven's style could be enumerated, but space restricts us to the mention of only a few.[1] He shows a predilection for sequencing at the interval of a fourth above : for example : —

From the C minor violin sonata (Op. 30, No. 2) : —

No. 104

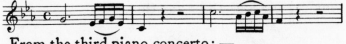

From the third piano concerto : —

No. 105

---

[1] The reader who wishes to pursue the subject further is referred to the article of Hans Gál already mentioned, and to Paul Mies's book *Die Bedeutung der Skizzen Beethovens zur Erkenntnis seines Stiles* (1925).

From the *Fidelio* overture: —

No. 106

Again, he feels, under certain circumstances, an irresistible impulse to dispense with a preliminary up-beat and, under others, to add an up-beat or modify the original one; it all depends on the general character of the melody. Thus in the Sketch Book the theme of the slow movement of the sonata in E minor (Op. 90) : —

No. 107

begins with another kind of up-beat: —

No. 108

The sketch for a melody in the fifth quartet (in A major) of Opus 18 begins thus: —

No. 109

which in the final version is altered to:

No. 110

In the sketch, the *Hammerklavier* sonata began thus: —

No. 111

The curt up-beat with which the sonata actually begins was an afterthought: it probably came from some such mood in the composer as prompted the similar " boring-in " up-beat (as a German writer calls it) in the first and second bars of the *Pathétique* sonata, of the March in the piano sonata in A major (Op. 101), and of the first movement of the sonata in C minor (Op. 111).

The strangest case of this unconscious urge towards an up-beat commencement in certain circumstances is that of the adagio of the *Hammerklavier* sonata. Beethoven's pupil Ries tells us of his astonishment at a letter he received one day in 1819 from Beethoven. The huge sonata was already engraved, and Ries was daily expecting the announcement of its publication, when Beethoven wrote to him that a bar containing the two notes A and C sharp was to be prefixed to the bar with which the adagio had commenced. " Two notes to be added to so great and so carefully wrought a work, six months after it was completed! " says Ries in amazement. He could not know, as we do, how subject Beethoven was to the unconscious in him. The original impulse to add a " curtain," as Hugo Riemann aptly calls a preliminary bar of this kind, had probably been suppressed during the composition of the adagio. But though suppressed it could not be killed; and when at last it rose into Beethoven's upper consciousness he *had* to add the up-beat bar, even though the sonata was then on the point of being published.

V

THE operation of the unconscious in Beethoven, however, can be most clearly seen in those sketches for the *Eroica* that have been published and so ably commented on by Nottebohm. Here, more than anywhere else, do we get that curious feeling that in his greatest works Beethoven was "possessed"— the mere human instrument through which a vast musical design realized itself in all its marvellous logic. As we study this Sketch Book we have the conviction that his mind did not proceed from the particular to the whole, but began, in some curious way, with the whole and then worked back to the particular. Apparently, here and elsewhere, he is anxiously seeking for the themes upon which to begin to construct a movement; and every one has heard of the many changes through which a theme would go in the sketch books before Beethoven hit upon the final acceptable form of it. But to assume that it was out of the themes that the movement grew is probably to see the process from the wrong end. From the Sketch Books, we get the impression that in some queer subconscious way the movement possessed him as a whole before he began to think out the details; and the long and painful search for the themes was simply an effort, not to find work-able atoms out of which he could construct a musical edifice according to the conventions of symphonic form, but to reduce an already existing nebula, in which that edifice was implicit, to the atom, and then, by the orderly arrangement of these atoms, to make the implicit explicit. This was not Mozart's way. With Mozart the themes are the first things to be thought of: the composer invents these for their own sake, and then manipulates them according partly to his fancy, partly to rule. With Beethoven we feel that the music has gone through the reverse process, that the themes are not the generators of the mass of the music, but are themselves rather the condensation of this. One is reminded of Pascal's profound saying, "You would not have sought me unless you had already found me." Beethoven's search for his themes is a kind of application of that subtle phenomenon of religious experience to music; the search is merely the attempt to bring into the open, and give definite visible shape to, something that is already active and potent, though invisible and only dimly sensed. Beethoven's difficulty was precisely what Mozart and other composers found easiest of all. The agonies through which he sometimes went in the composition of a work were the result of this terrific effort at condensation of the unconsciously previsioned whole into its consciously isolated germ-themes;

(The numbering of the bars is mine.)

once these had been found they almost spontane-ously regenerated the whole with comparatively little effort on his part. Nothing can be more mis-leading than to suppose that Beethoven and Mo-zart both constructed in the same way a sym-phonic movement out of a "first main tune" and "a second main tune." The mental processes in-volved were fundamentally different in the two cases.

For the whole of the music of the sketches for the *Eroica* that Nottebohm has reproduced the reader must be referred to his book — the second of his publications of this kind.[1] Here I can indulge myself in the luxury of quoting only the first of what Notte-bohm calls the "Four Great Sketches" (in addition to which there are many smaller ones). (See No. 112.)

To assist the reader to follow the argument with the minimum of trouble, it will be as well to quote here the main thematic material of the first section of the first movement of the *Eroica*. The first sub-ject, which, for convenience of reference, we will call A, runs thus : —

---

[1] Nottebohm's original editions of 1865 and 1880 are now difficult to procure; but both books have lately been re-issued in one volume by Breitkopf & Härtel — *Zwei Skizzenbücher von Beethoven aus den Jahren 1801 bis 1803, beschrieben . . . von Gustav Nottebohm*, edited by Paul Mies (1924).

No. 113

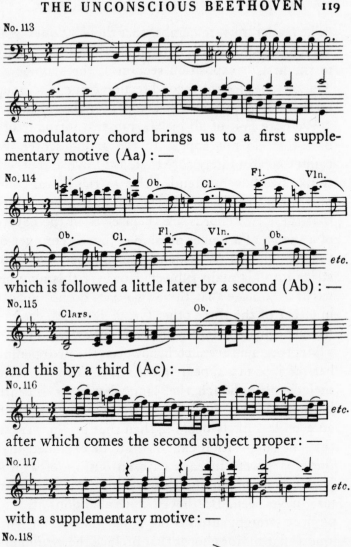

A modulatory chord brings us to a first supplementary motive (Aa) : —

No. 114

which is followed a little later by a second (Ab) : —

No. 115

and this by a third (Ac) : —

No. 116

after which comes the second subject proper : —

No. 117

with a supplementary motive : —

No. 118

(The reader must remember that these " Four Great Sketches " and the cognate smaller ones relate only to the first or exposition section of the symphony. The sketches for the second section come in a group by themselves; so do the sketches for the third.)

We note first of all in No. 112 two introductory bars that do not appear in the actual score. We cannot be absolutely sure that, as Grove and others think, Beethoven intended this as the literal commencement of the work; there is just a possibility that these two chords are themselves in the nature of a sketch of a longer preamble, just a reminder of the modulation by which the composer meant to strike into his main subject. However this may be, we have to note that these two bars do not appear in either of the three other Great Sketches, each of which begins outright with the familiar No. 113. In a later fragmentary sketch, however, the two opening bars of No. 112 appear in a slightly different form melodically, though the same dominant seventh harmony is preserved. This variant seems, in itself, an even less likely opening than that in No. 112, so that the supposition cannot quite be excluded that these bars were in each case an outline of a projected short preamble. But whatever his first plan may have been, Beethoven now abandons it, and plunges straight into his big E flat theme. The two loud E flat major chords that preface the symphony as we now have it seem to have been added after the

movement was fully worked out; and we are irresistibly reminded of the later insertion of a preliminary bar before the adagio in the *Hammerklavier* sonata.

It will be seen that this First Great Sketch contains, in embryo, practically the whole of the thematic material of the exposition section with the
exception of the main second subject — No. 113 in
the third and following bars, a hint of No. 118 in
bars 24 ff., a bare suggestion of No. 114 in bars 44 ff.,
No. 115 in bars 55 ff., and No. 116 in bars 59 ff.
From this relative completeness Nottebohm conjectures — or rather asserts positively — that " when
this was written down, the work was already in its
advanced stage, and therefore must have been begun in another place; it is possible that what we
have here is just the first connected Great Sketch for
the first section, a collocation of the smaller sketches
made in an earlier Sketch Book." I see no particular
reason to assume this; it is quite conceivable that
this First Great Sketch is Beethoven's first attempt
to fix on paper his vague conception of a symphonic
movement.[1] One or two of his conversations give us
a hint that he dimly saw a work as a whole before
beginning to labour at the details of it. On this point,
however, more will be said later.

In the Second Great Sketch, Aa has become a

---

[1] Which, of course, does not preclude the possibility of his having made
innumerable " sketches " in his head.

little better defined: Beethoven is still fumbling with it melodically, but he has hit upon the characteristic dotted-crotchet-quaver-crotchet of No. 114. In the Third Great Sketch the motive is very nearly as we have it in the score, even to the modulatory G flat in the tenth bar of No. 114. Nottebohm conjectures that Beethoven must have found the motive in its first form (i.e., as shown in No. 112) unsatisfactory for his purpose, because these notes of equal value did not sufficiently separate the level crotchet-values of the main theme and of Ab. But surely it is a gratuitous assumption that Beethoven ever planned Aa to run on the lines of bars 43-54 of No. 112. Is it not more probable that No. 112 was just the first rough jotting of a scheme that was vaguely hovering before him in its totality, and which he was anxious to fix on paper in its broadest outlines as soon as possible? Probably what he was most concerned about at this stage was not so much to settle the actual themes as to define the general *balance* of the parts of the picture, in the way that a painter will sometimes do, leaving great gaps between the corners, to be filled in later. I take it that in Beethoven's extraordinary mind the *whole* of the movement already existed, in some curious way, before the details were clear to him. He did not, as I have said, begin, like Mozart, with definite themes,[1] from

---

[1] The reader will bear in mind that I am here discussing only the great symphonic movements. In the movements in variation form, his improvisations, and elsewhere, Beethoven would of course make the theme his starting-point.

which the movement almost automatically evolved itself; he began with a dim vision of the totality of what the movement was to express, and then had to dig his themes out of this, very much as a sculptor sees the statue in the mass of marble, and gets at it by cutting away as much of the latter as he does not want. The ideal form for each theme could be attended to later; meanwhile the important thing was to make a general survey of the field, and to fix the main lines, masses and proportions.

Since the musician does his designing in part by means of balance and contrast of keys, Beethoven had first of all to fix the sequence of these. This we see him hurriedly doing in the First Great Sketch. He gets his main subject in E flat,[1] whence he naturally gravitates towards some subsidiary matter in B flat. He knows also, though as yet only vaguely, what he wants in the way of thematic material — something like Aa, Ab, and Ac. Of these Ab gives him practically no trouble at all, and Ac comparatively little. But he is almost completely in the dark, as yet, as to what Aa is to be thematically. He has, in fact, already become a trifle confused in the bars following 36 in No. 112. Nothing definite *can* emerge from all this, and by the time he has reached bar 43 he cannot at all fix his image, *thematically*. But in the matter of tonality, which is so essential a part

---

[1] His certainty as to this one theme from the very commencement perhaps bears out the theory that at some time or other, somewhere or other, he must have heard the overture to Mozart's *Bastien et Bastienne*.

of that general design from which we imagine him to have proceeded, he knows beyond a doubt what he wants — some phrase with a descending curve, to contrast with the feeling of ascent that has been predominant so far, and with a definite physiognomy in the matter of tonality. He hastily jots down as much as he is sure of at the moment — the droop of the melody, the vital intrusion of G flat at a certain point, and the later restoration of G natural to its rights. All this is, in essence, precisely as it will appear later in the score. He does not even trouble to make a dash at the notes of the motive, as he has done in the other cases; he jots down his idea in a sort of shorthand, leaving six bars blank. I do not think we are in the least justified in assuming, with Nottebohm, that he ever seriously thought of working out this particular motive in crotchets. It may be added that in a later small sketch he once more uses the G flat just as a shorthand reminder, leaving a number of bars blank as before. In the Second Great Sketch the theme at last becomes clearly defined.

We have various little indications that he dimly — subconsciously — saw his movement as a whole before he had any more than a vague idea of the shape the thematic fragments would need to be. Nottebohm justly draws attention to the modulation to the key of D flat in bar 75 of No. 112, and to the fact that this key, which is the remotest tonality suggested in the Sketch, is also the remotest tonality reached in the whole section. In some of the later sketches he did not make this modulation, so that his final adoption of it is a reversion to his original idea — the " pull " of the unconscious within him. Well may Nottebohm speak of the " prophetic significance " of the First Great Sketch.

It is in the Second Great Sketch that the second subject proper (No. 117) appears for the first time, but in a curiously inchoate form: —

No. 119

while in the Third Great Sketch it appears thus: —

No. 120

(In both examples, of course, the reader will supply the necessary flats before the B's and E's.)

In the Fourth Great Sketch the theme draws nearer to its final form in some respects, though in others diverging further from it than the two earlier attempts had done; and it is not until we come to a later small sketch that it comes out right, miraculously so as it seems. But I find it difficult to believe that Beethoven stumbled, as it were, on themes of this kind by a sort of accident, fumbling helplessly with all kinds of commonplaces until, almost by a process of exhaustion of the various possibilities, he hit upon the right form. I think it more probable that, as I have conjectured with regard to Aa in the First Great Sketch, he was at first intent, now and then, not so much on hammering out his theme as on fixing proportions, modulations, and so on to his satisfaction; rather than hold up this part of his task in order to settle on the precise notes of a theme he would be content with a rough blocking out of this. To compare his procedure again with that of the painter, it is as if he were to draw the rough outline of a head in its proper place and with its proper proportion in the design, and splash in a suggestion of its value in the colour scheme, leaving the filling-in of the features to a later time.

Other parts of the sketches confirm this theory. He can be seen to have realized, at a certain point, that a certain breaking of the rhythm, perhaps by means of syncopations or cross times, is desirable; so a rough hint of the rhythm desired is put on paper, to be worked out melodically and harmonically later. Sometimes the final form of a figure does not appear at all in the sketches; the inference is that he regarded the seemingly clumsy attempts to fix the figure in the sketches as mere reminders of its place and function in the general design, and that

when all this was satisfactorily settled he had not
much difficulty in finding the ideal melodic form for
the rhythmic or harmonic idea.

That he thus worked from the periphery to the
centre of his vision, instead of, as the text-books
would have us believe, inventing germ-themes and
then developing them, is proved by two instances
that at first sight would seem to contradict this
theory. At two points the sketches seem to show him
to be intent on a detail for its own sake — to be hammering away at it before he has reached the place
where it is ultimately to be used. But here again it
is evident, on closer consideration, that the general
design, though not yet noted down, is latent in his
mind, and that he wants to settle the details not because they pleased him in and by themselves, but
because they are vital points in the totality of his
plan.

The first case is that of the lovely episode that
appears in the working-out section: —

No. 121

In the first movement of the *Eroica* the second
main subject (No. 117) plays a singularly small
part. Without attempting to read too definite a pro-
gramme into the movement, no one who under-
stands Beethoven can doubt that at the back of the

notes is a train of thought that remotely corresponds to what we can only call by the crude name of a "poetic idea." The work is "absolute" music, in that its logic is that of the musical faculty *per se* functioning at its finest; yet assuredly all these affirmations, and doubts, and reservations, and bursts of temper, and convulsive gestures, and sudden transitions to softer moods are the outcome of a train of thought that ran within the musical one, as a nerve runs in its sheath. It is from the workings of this other train of thought that the tender, wistful episode in E minor has come; [1] it is a divagation of the "poetic" no less than of the musical vision within him. Nottebohm, with the whole of the Sketch Book before him, tells us that "for the second section [the working-out] there are many small sketches, and two that cover the whole of the section. . . . From the first of the former it is clear that, before the second part is otherwise worked out, he had decided on introducing the lyrical episode, and in E minor. The direction of the modulation was thus already indicated, if not, as yet, its actual route."

The episode was a bridge, and it does not need to be insisted on that a bridge cannot be built without reference to the land at either end of it. Beethoven,

---

[1] It is curious that in all the sketches he writes in only the lower voice of the two-part theme.

that is to say, must have had the surrounding design fairly complete in his mind before he began to design his bridge. That this was so becomes even more evident from the second of the two cases above mentioned — the famous entry of the horn with the first subject (No. 113) under a kind of tremolo in the violins, the result being that dissonance that so gravely troubled the consciences of theorists and conductors in the early days — troubled some of them, indeed, to the extent of making them alter the A flat in the second violins to G: —

No. 122

These bars form the transition between the second and third sections of the movement; they are followed by a couple of bars' crescendo on the dominant seventh, leading into a fortissimo resumption of the first subject as at the commencement of the symphony; the ship has weathered the storm, and now makes for the harbour under full sail.

The sketches show that this manner of transition from the second to the final section was decided upon long in advance of the writing of either of these sections. He evidently wanted a startling effect of a particular kind — some modulations out of the main keys of the work, a tentative settling upon the harmony of the dominant seventh, a mysterious entry of the " heroic " theme against a chord irreconcilable with it, a moment's gathering up of the forces, then a final plunge into the energetic " heroic " motive as the commencement of the recapitulation section. Unquestionably the point is " programmatic." Beethoven, however, was at first uncertain as to how to make the desired effect; as usual, he saw the whole before he was clear as to the details. He begins with a cumulus (./.) on the A flat alone: —

No. 123

and brings the theme in twice, which is an excess of zeal. In a later sketch he substitutes for the A flat a single D, thus making a still harsher dissonance. Later he rejects this solution of his problem and decides on B flat and A flat, as they are now in the score, but still weakens his effect somewhat by overelaboration. Still later he hits upon practically the present form of the passage, with the two succeeding bars of the dominant seventh. Then he has his doubts again; and this time, in place of the cumulus and the dissonance he tries a long run (presumably in the violins) ending in the " heroic " theme. He must have soon been convinced that this would not do at all, for he resumes his experiments with the cumulus until he has settled on the final form for the passage. But however he may diverge at this point or that from his original idea, in essence it remains the same; never, as Nottebohm points out, does he so much as dream of softening the dissonance into a consonance, as the earlier conductors and theorists would fain have done with the passage. And no one with any knowledge of the workings of Beethoven's mind can doubt that Nottebohm is right in saying that it is perfectly obvious that the passage had, for the composer, " a symbolical significance."

VI

IN various other cases, that need not be gone into
in detail here, we have evidence that Beethoven
did not evolve the mass of a movement of this kind
from consciously invented themes, but arrived at
the themes by a slow process of condensation from
a more or less dimly previsioned mass. It would be
an exaggeration, of course, to say that he never
worked in the reverse fashion, after the manner of
other composers. But in his greater works, and especially his first movements, the process seems to have
been that I have tried to describe. He begins with
a nebula, out of which he gradually condenses the
vital atoms that are to be his themes. Frequently
it is a mainly rhythmical shape that is hovering
somewhere in the depths of the unconscious in him.
He begins by roughing it out as a rhythm, and only
after several experiments finds the melodic form
that was predestined to give the rhythm flesh and
blood. At other times it will be an effect of key contrast that he foresees a long way ahead as an essential of his design; thus the statement of the
" heroic " theme in F major immediately after the
commencement of the third section (in bar 11) was

decided upon while he was working at the second section. At the same time he forecast the beginning of the coda.

It is in his fast movements, in which Beethoven's genius is most fully realized, that he is most plainly taken possession of by a subconscious force that imposes its own logic on him in its own peculiar way. It may be that one reason for the relatively inferior strength of the generality of his slow movements is that in these he worked more from the centre to the periphery than he did in his fast movements. In the latter, as I have suggested, he got at his themes by a slow condensation from a nebula; in the former he more consciously made his theme at the beginning. The main themes of his fast movements are, in many cases, in themselves quite insignificant — a point that was noted by some of his contemporaries. Had the symphonies to which they belong never been written, had we only the themes themselves in a Sketch Book, we would probably not give a second glance at such seemingly inexpressive and impossible fragments as the first subjects of the Third, Fifth and Ninth Symphonies. It is not they that make the movement; it is the movement that, when we emerge from it and look back to its starting-point, gives them their stupendous significance. In his andantes he works on longer, more song-like themes, that develop straightforwardly from their original quasi-lyrical germ. The seminal potentialities of this germ are soon exhausted. Beethoven cannot go on developing from it indefinitely, as he appears to be able to do with the germs of his fast movements; the lyrical flight soon comes to an end, and the composer is generally driven to variations upon the theme.

We have the feeling that he more consciously *made* his slow movements, while his fast ones were rather made for him by the unconscious within him; hence the variety and the power of the latter, and the uniformity of mood and the comparative lack of technical resource in the former. He had, one almost ventures to assert, only the one mood to express in his andantes, and it depended on the accident of the moment whether he showed himself as a genius or as a talent in them. If the incandescence were too low, he sank to a talent; but nowhere is he merely a talent in the fast movements of his prime. What it is precisely that makes the difference between two such movements as the adagio of the C minor violin sonata (Op. 30, No. 2) and the adagio of the G major violin sonata (Op. 96) we cannot say; all we know is that the former is the work of a talent and the latter of a genius, even if not such a genius as Beethoven can show himself to be on other occasions. A movement like the andante of the B flat trio (Op. 97) is on the border-line between talent and genius. If earnestness and fine moral purpose were of themselves sufficient in art, some of Beethoven's slow movements would be greater than the modern world can conscientiously pronounce them to be. But these qualities are not sufficient, as we know from a comparison of Wordsworth in his pedestrian moments with Wordsworth in his moments of illumination; the excellent sentiment needs to be kindled to a peculiar incandescence before it becomes art of the finest kind. The text of Beethoven's discourse in some of his slow movements is unimpeachable; the preacher's earnestness is beyond dispute. But because the final incandescence is not attained in the expression he remains just a preacher, not a seer and a magician as he is in the greater andantes.

Nor is Beethoven "possessed" in such movements as the finale of the *Eroica;* he is there a composer of ordinary genius building up his music in the ordinary way with occasional flashes of a genius that is extraordinary. Nottebohm tells us, from the evidence of the Sketch Book, that "the composition of the finale of the symphony took relatively less time than that of the other movements. Beethoven was quite clear from the beginning both as to his theme and the general form." Naturally: he is simply planning, quite consciously, a theme and variations. The conceptual and evolutionary processes are the reverse of those in the first movement. There he had begun with a vague vision of a whole that had to be slowly differentiated into its thematic details; in the finale he has merely to choose his theme and proceed to the elaboration of it. But in the scherzo we see once more the experimental search for the right starting-point, the attempt to condense the atom out of the nebula. The first form of the theme runs thus: —

No. 124

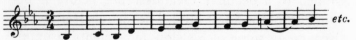

Later it takes on more of the appearance of the theme as we now have it. But, incredible as it seems to us to-day, there is apparently no doubt that when Beethoven began the movement he intended it to be a minuet more or less in the older style; [1] and it puzzles us that he should ever have conceived the idea of a minuet in connection with such a work. He was set right by the unconscious logic of things within him — that logic which, as I have tried to show, sometimes takes hold of a prose writer's first idea and turns it round into something else, or that makes a character in a novel sometimes develop in a way its creator did not originally intend, as nov-

---

[1] *Note to 2nd edition.* I leave this passage — which expresses the general opinion on the matter — as it stood in the first edition. On reflection, however, it seems at least as probable that all that Beethoven meant by the " M " (Menuetto?) at the commencement of the sketches was a movement in triple time, occupying in the symphony the place traditionally allotted to the Minuet. On the other hand, his marking the theme *Presto* in one of the later sketches certainly seems to indicate a change of view in regard to it. It is impossible now to settle the point conclusively one way or the other.

elists of genius have assured us has frequently been
the case with them. After a bit of uneasy fumbling
with the idea adumbrated in No. 124, Beethoven
suddenly hits upon this:—

No. 125

which is very nearly the theme as it appears in the
score. But though the differences between No. 124
and No. 125 seem at first sight trifling, they are
packed with significance. The marking of *Presto* indicates a complete change in Beethoven's way of regarding his first conception of the movement; while
the new turn given to the theme by the substitution
of B flat for C as the second note (involving as it
does a total change in the swing of the melody) is, as
Nottebohm indicates, a vital point of difference.
What has happened is that the basic conception has
suddenly switched over from that of a minuet to
that of a scherzo, in obedience to an unconscious
logic in the composer. His fundamental idea having
thus been clarified for him, the work of beating the
theme into shape proceeds rapidly. And the clari-
fication automatically brings with it a further
change of purpose. What would have done well
enough as a trio to his minuet will not do at all as a
trio to this scherzo, and Beethoven has to abandon
his first sketch and set out in search of a trio theme
that will cohere with his new conception.

VII

AT the conclusion of his examination of the *Eroica* sketches Nottebohm takes up the psychological problem suggested by them. He sees, as others had done, that Beethoven, in his great movements, never lost sight of the whole when engaged in the elaboration of the parts; but Nottebohm fails, I think, to see the problem quite as it is. The solution of it that I have ventured to put forward — that when his marvellous genius was working at its best he was possessed by the totality of a conception thrown up from the unconscious within him, and that the sketches represent the effort to separate this totality into its basic atoms — can in the nature of the case be only a suggestion; but it is one that, with our modern knowledge of the part played by the unconscious in artistic creation, will seem less incredible than it might have done to an earlier age. We know the curious way in which the unconscious worked in Hugo Wolf — how he would read a poem and brood upon it overnight, but without making any attempt to translate it into music, and then sleep upon it and in the morning find that the music had made itself, and that so completely, with such unerring logic, that all that Wolf had to do was to fix the notes upon paper as fast as his pen would let him. We have, again, the case of Coleridge and *Kubla Khan;* the poem makes itself in a dream state (in this case induced by opium), shows itself, in a waking state, to the upper consciousness, and needs only to be noted down.

But obviously Beethoven was something more than an instrument of the unconscious. He sought consciously for his themes, and did a good deal of conscious manipulation of them and designing with them. There was, in fact, a something else that Nottebohm calls the " agent," and to which he gives the more specific title of " the reflective reason." " Reflection of itself, however," he says, " is cold; it is not creative; it is incapable of generating beauty. It is not, and cannot be, the chief thing in art. The first thing with Beethoven was imagination; the last thing was also imagination, but imagination shot through with reflection. The two faculties worked separately and in alternation; the unconscious allied itself with the considered. The reason tested, sifted, pointed out defects, while the creative force gave anything that the reason asked for, and thereby asserted the freedom of its own operations and its own overlordship. It was protected by a charm against every cramping influence that might threaten its existence. With Beethoven it was not as with other mortals, in whom the imagination sleeps while the ' work ' is being done. With Beethoven the imagination worked all the time unweakened, and indeed often took its highest flight at the last moment. This suppleness of imagination and formalism, this coolness, circumspection, and continual patience during the course of the work, is part of the quality upon which the greatness of Beethoven depends, without which Beethoven would not have been Beethoven. I say a part, for other qualities went to make Beethoven's greatness — qualities which, with some limitation regarding the qualities we have already ascribed to the imagination, we may sum up under the name of genius. Between these and the other qualities there is a distinction. These are inborn capacities, the others are acquired qualities, which pertain not to the individual and the native constitution but to person and to character. It is these latter qualities whose functioning we see in the sketches. In the Sketch Book the accent falls on the work that lies between the original total idea and the completed creation."

This, however, does not quite elucidate the subject. Everyone knows that along with what we vaguely call " inspiration " in art there must go a certain amount of what Nottebohm calls " reflective reason " and to which Tchaikovski gave the name of " head work." Tchaikovski, answering a correspondent who wanted to know how he wrote his music, said, in effect, that the main idea and the themes of a work came to him in the quasi-somnambulistic state that the world calls "inspiration." Virtually whatever he did in this state was right, or seemed to him right. But, he went on to say, the composer could not remain permanently in this rapt state. Necessarily, in the course of a long work which would have to be laid down and taken up again many times, it would often be impossible to recapture the somnambulistic mood; and then the composer would have to rely on "head work" — skilled craftsmanship and taste and experience and "reflective reason" performing as best they could the functions of the imagination. Tchaikovski recognized that the passages written in these moments of lower incandescence were likely to be weaker than those conceived in the somnambulistic state. "All that is good but superfluous," he said to another correspondent, "we call padding," and he cited Beethoven as the supreme example of a composer in whose music padding is least evident: "could anyone show me a bar of the *Eroica* — which is very lengthy — that could be called superfluous, or any portion that could really be omitted as padding?" He modestly contrasted himself with the giant in this respect: "I shall go to my grave without having produced anything really perfect in form. There is frequently padding in my works; to an experienced eye the stitches show in my seams, but I cannot help it."

Busoni has attempted the reconciliation of these

two processes of "heart" and "head," as they would be styled in popular language. "No more than a singer can sing all in one breath can a composer invent in a breath [*aus einem Guss*, at a single casting]. The continuation is achieved by means of connecting matter, sequences, modulations, contrasts, unfortunately also by an interspersion of conventional formulæ. If anyone doubts this, let him try for himself. Nevertheless 'inspiration' [*Eingebung*] is as necessary to the seemingly conventional spinning-out of the theme as to its invention. The actuator of this organism is the idea, the 'regulator' is the instinct of proportion, the contents-giver is the soul, the expression-bearer is the heart, the worker-out is the understanding." But this still leaves us with two processes that, whatever names we give to them, seem to be distinct — "inspiration" and "head work."

The peculiarity of Beethoven seems to have been that in his greatest music head work was carried on at the same level of incandescence as inspiration, and that over a long composition that must have been laid down and taken up again many times in the course of several months. His technique was as "inspired" as his "inspiration." The unconscious, which admittedly is the generating force for the unexpected, incalculable, inexplicable felicities that we call inspirations, seems to have taken charge also, in Beethoven, of those more consciously forged links between the scattered inspirations that we call head work. It was the one supremely logical musical faculty that was functioning all the time; and it is this that accounts for his way of commencing, as I have conjectured, with a vague general idea of the totality of a movement, solidifying the nebula at certain decisive points into themes — a slow and painful process — and then proceeding with comparative ease to extend this solidification over the whole field of the nebula, till in the end the all-embracing, all-vivifying logic that was at first only dimly explicit to himself becomes magnificently explicit to the whole world.

The records we have of his method of composition, and especially his own references to them, confirm this view. Schubert's friend Karl Johann Braun von Braunthal gives us a description of Beethoven that suggests the somnambulist. Braun von Braunthal and a number of other people were in a restaurant one day when Beethoven entered. (It was during the last years of his life.) " Everyone was filled with the deepest reverential awe [*Ehrfurcht*] when he entered. A man of middle height, very solidly built, with a veritably leonine head surrounded by a grey mane, and bright piercing eyes that wandered all around him; he moved about uncertainly, as if in a dream. He sat down before a glass of beer, smoked a long pipe, and closed his eyes. When spoken to, or, as more often happened, shouted at by

one of his acquaintances, he raised his eyelids like
an eagle startled from its slumber, broke into a sad
smile, handed his interlocutor a notebook and pen-
cil, and asked him, in that screeching voice that
is characteristic of the deaf, to write his question
down. . . . Now and then he took from his breast
pocket another and thicker book, in which he wrote
with half-closed eyes. 'What is he writing?' I asked
my neighbour [Schubert] one evening. 'He is composing,' was the answer. 'But he is writing words,
not notes.' 'That is his method; he usually indicates
in words the course of the ideas in a composition,
at the most adding a few notes in between. . . . Art
has already become science to him; he knows what
he can do, and his imagination obeys his unfathom-
able reflection.'" This last phrase, I take it, was
Schubert's way of saying that in Beethoven the
" imagination " or "inspiration " controlled also
the " head work."

Czerny, who was in close association with him for
many years, tells us that " he often carried the idea
of a composition about with him for years before he
began to work it out on paper." He assures us also
that the main theme of the *Eroica* ran thus originally: —

No. 126

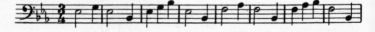

" as it appears at the end of the first movement "
(which is not absolutely correct). Whether Czerny's
memory has served him faithfully here or not we
cannot be sure; but if he is right, the fact is worth
noting.

Beethoven's pupil Ries, who also saw him under
intimate circumstances for many years, tells us that
on one of their walks together in the country Beethoven " muttered and howled the whole time, without emitting any definite notes. When I asked him
what he was doing he answered, ' A theme for the
last allegro of the sonata [the *Appassionata*] has
occurred to me.' When we reached the house he ran,
without stopping to take off his hat, to the piano. I
sat in a corner, and he soon forgot all about me. He
then raved and roared [*tobte*] for at least an hour
over the new and beautiful finale. At last he got up;
he was astonished to find me still there, and said, ' I
cannot give you a lesson to-day: I must go on working.' "

Apparently during the walk he had been engaged
in precipitating the theme out of the vague mass of
ideas that held it *in posse*.

To Louis Schlösser, Kapellmeister in Darmstadt,
and himself a composer, Beethoven thus described
his own method of working: " I carry my ideas
about with me for a long time — often a very long
time — before I write them down." (This would
seem to confirm the conjecture that the sketches

represent anything but the first conceptual stage of a work; rather are they the first attempt to fix in notes the main "moments," the general proportions, and the modulatory scheme of a conception that had already been turned over a thousand times in his head.) "My memory is so accurate that I am certain of not forgetting, even in the course of several years, a theme that has once occurred to me. I alter many things, reject and try again, until I am satisfied; then begins in my head the working-out in the broad, in the narrow, in the height, in the depth; and since I am conscious of what I want, the fundamental idea never leaves me; it mounts, it grows, I see before my mind the picture in its whole extent, as it were in a single projection [*in einem Gusse*], and nothing remains to be done but the work of writing it down, that gets along quickly according to the time I can spare for it, for I sometimes have several works in hand at once, but I never confuse one with another."

Here again the impression given is that Beethoven did a vast amount of work at a movement in his head before ever he began to try to fix the ideas on paper, and that the Sketch Books represent not the first but a relatively advanced stage in the making of the music. Perhaps the suggestion put forward in the foregoing pages is permissible — that Beethoven did not, as most composers do, begin with an "idea," an "inspiration," that first appears in the form of a theme, which has then to be developed by " head work," with as strong an admixture of inspiration as the composer can command, but started with a vague general sense of the totality of the movement, gradually condensed this into vital structural material, and finally re-wrought this into a whole that was the first indefinite conception made perfectly definite. This procedure has little in common with that of the composer who plans say, a symphonic poem, or even a symphonic movement of the " absolute music " kind. There also, of course, a general idea must antedate the particular themes : Strauss, for instance, in *Ein Heldenleben*, had the general idea of a picture of a hero's life before he began inventing themes to represent this or that phase of the life. But cases of this kind represent merely the settling upon the shape and the dimensions of a frame before proceeding to the business of filling it ; having once decided on the frame and on the main lines on which the picture is to be constructed, the composer first of all sets to work to invent a theme expressive of each of the main " moments " of the picture, and then links them up. With Beethoven, as I see the matter, the case was the reverse of this. He was not certain of the whole in advance in the way that Strauss would be certain in advance of all that his scheme for a picture of a hero's life was to contain. Beethoven was in the first place only vaguely subconscious of a whole ; this vague concept had to be

M

gradually brought into the upper consciousness; and this was effected by the slow condensation of the vague mass into a few basic themes, which were less invented than discovered, as the unconscious bit by bit emerged into the conscious. And the unconscious controlled the "reflective reason" in Beethoven as it has never done in any other musician. He seems, indeed, in the Sketch Books, to be consciously and coolly manipulating his material; but it is much in the way that the man who believes he is exercising his free will is often only following a line marked out for him by forces that function too far down in his subconsciousness for him to be aware of them.

INDEX

INDEX